JEMIMA PARRY-JONES'
FALCONRY

JEMIMA PARRY-JONES'
FALCONRY
CARE, CAPTIVE BREEDING
AND CONSERVATION

Revised edition

David & Charles

Danny

(Frontispiece)
My father, Phillip Glasier, flying Islay, his female
Harris Hawk. He has permission from many kind
landowners to fly over thousands of acres

All photographs, unless otherwise specified, were supplied by
The National Birds of Prey Centre

A DAVID & CHARLES BOOK

© Jemima Parry-Jones 1988, 1993

First published 1988
Reprinted 1989, 1991
Revised edition 1993

A catalogue record for this book is available from the British
Library.

ISBN 0 7153 0105 5

Typeset by Typesetters (Birmingham) Ltd
and printed in Great Britain by Butler & Tanner Ltd
for David & Charles
Brunel House   Newton Abbot   Devon

CONTENTS

To Jo

INTRODUCTION

To anyone who is interested in birds of prey, I must seem incredibly lucky to be owner of such a collection of raptors, and to have them around me at all times. While I sit in my office writing this book, I can see through the window the odd falcon or eagle flying outside, during one of the demonstrations. I can hear the cry of the African Fish Eagle and often an irate falcon calling as one of the eagles goes over her pen. If I continue writing on into the evening, the owls in their pens start calling and, more exciting, the local wild owls add their voices to the chorus. Sadly I haven't heard a Barn Owl for some years, but one day they will come back.

I am also lucky in that I was asked by the publishers to write this book, rather than having to find someone willing to publish it after I had completed it. I will admit, though, that probably I would not have written it at all had they not asked me. Sitting down to write a book is a daunting task, particularly if you find it difficult to sit still for any length of time anyway, and when there are so many attractions outside that you really would much rather get on with. However, over the years I have answered so many questions, and written so many letters to people all over the world, that it really was time to save my voice, time and typewriter ribbon and put my thoughts into a book instead—so here it is.

I hope that it will answer many of those questions. It is for all those people who care passionately about birds of prey, and their welfare. It will help in the captive breeding field, whether breeding birds of prey for falconry, scientific research, captive release schemes or just for fun. It is not really a technical book on how to become a falconer, and on flying birds—the best manual on falconry for beginners has already been written by my father, Phillip Glasier. This book should interest those who are considering taking up falconry as a sport; parts may well annoy the hell out of some people but, as a good friend of mine often says when giving me anything—enjoy!

Falconry, having remained almost unchanged for centuries, has undergone considerable changes over the last twenty-five years, for a number of different reasons. An increasing number of people are wanting to know more about the sport, and about how they can take part. Non-indigenous species of raptors which had not been used before in Britain have, over the last three decades, been imported, flown and captive bred. Some have now become more widely used than the indigenous species.

Telemetry—the use of radio transmitters and receivers—which help the falconer find a bird should he or she become lost, have meant that birds can now be flown at a higher weight and in areas that previously were considered too enclosed for safe flying. Veterinary medicine has improved immeasurably and now broken limbs can be repaired, and illnesses diagnosed, understood and treated. Because of this, and many other factors, falconers on the whole have become a great deal better at looking after their birds. New legislation has been brought in to cover all birds of prey and falconry. This has caused large-scale changes in the obtaining and keeping of birds.

That legislation, combined with an upsurge of interest in the sport, has rendered birds far less easily available, and much more expensive. Many an older falconer will complain that he or she (and me, I'm afraid to say!) can remember when Goshawks were £15 and £20 to buy. These birds are now reaching four-figure sums, although I think that the price is over-high at the moment and should drop once we get more successful at breeding this most difficult of species. Nevertheless, it should also be remembered by those people that at the time Goshawks were £20, petrol was 5/6d (27p) a gallon, and I bet that they would be pretty upset if they only got the same price today that they paid for their house twenty-five years ago! I am glad that Goshawks are no longer so accessible: the high price keeps them out of reach of many people who should not own such birds until they are more experienced falconers, and understand the different species a little better.

The most vital change as far as the future of falconry is concerned is the arrival of, and advances in, captive breeding. This means that in the long term falconry should become self-supporting, apart from the occasional addition of fresh blood for breeding. Captive breeding has, however, introduced its own problems, such as learning how to fly those birds which have been captive bred.

All these factors have changed falconry. I hope that this book will help people just starting the sport to think a little before doing so. Perhaps too, some of us who already partake could benefit from standing back and taking a good look at what we are doing.

I make no apologies for the style or the bluntness of this book. There is no intentional rudeness to any particular person; I just care greatly about my subject and about the birds.

JPJ
Newent, 1992

Black Sparrowhawk

1 THE NATIONAL
BIRDS OF PREY CENTRE

The Falconry Centre was started in 1966, opening to the public in May 1967 (in 1990 the name changed to The NBoPC). My father had talked about starting a centre for years and finally, encouraged by my mother and the rest of the family, decided to have a go. I had left school and so was available, and interested enough, to help full time. We moved up from Dorset in November '66 with twelve birds. We still have one of the original inmates, a Common Buzzard called Pete. She is on loan with a friend of mine in Derbyshire and for those of you with older birds, don't despair; at twenty-one years old she produced her first babies and hatched and reared them as well—not bad for an old lady! In those days, with no import restrictions, birds were easily available and by May 1967 we had about sixty birds. Martin Jones, now well known for his equipment (falconry wise) was at Cirencester Agriculture College at the time and used to come over regularly, collecting new arrivals at Gloucester station and helping out generally including building pens. He eventually ended up working here for some considerable time.

We used to get the oddest birds arrive here, who very often turned out to be nothing remotely resembling what had been advertised, and sometimes not even coming from the right continent. Some arrived in the most appalling condition and it took a great deal of time and effort to get them right again. One bird arrived in an old orange box. He was supposed to be a Roadside Hawk from America—she turned out to be a Yellow-billed Kite from Africa. She had been kept in heaven knows what, and had not one single feather on her wings, just bloodied flesh and bone. Needless to say she stayed, as did they all. She was put on jesses and placed on the lawn in the warm sun and offered a bath. She was very tame. About ten minutes later on checking her we noticed that she looked as if she was sitting much further away from the block than the leash length should have allowed—she was. There sitting next to her were the jesses, still complete but with no bird's legs in the straps. We tried twice more to keep jesses on her and then gave up. She couldn't fly and having quickly sorted out all the dogs and established that she was definitely boss she ambled about the garden and took up residence in the greenhouse. There she stayed with regular sorties about the garden until finally, two years later, when she had regrown all her feathers and started to get a little too adventurous, we tethered her in case she went near one of the trained eagles and got eaten for a quick snack. She is still with us and lives in one of our old pens with three other Yellow-billed Kites; all of them are females and they are all due to have a smart new pen one day, so that they can continue to lay hordes more infertile eggs.

Although her story ended well, we were generally quite pleased to see import restrictions come in, as many of the birds we saw were very sad cases indeed and often did not survive. I often wish that we had had the experience then, that we have now, as we would have been able to save more and would, I am sure, have bred from some of them. Many of the species that came in have subsequently become rarer in the wild, and we could have already achieved some valuable work with them had we had more knowledge.

By pure luck we have built up the whole collection slowly and so have learnt how to look after large numbers of birds without having a sudden influx. When you are caring for livestock that, in many cases, you only see for a very short period twice a day, you have to be able to look at the individual birds and say to yourself, 'That bird looks fine, all is well in the pen, it took its food well and the pair are getting on fine with one another, therefore I should not need to worry about them until they are checked again in the evening.' Many people may not even be able to check their birds twice a day in daylight hours during winter, and so even more experience is needed. We find that we 'listen' to the birds a great deal. Little or no notice is taken of the normal noises they all make, other than to note that they are making them, but if a noise that we don't normally hear is made, we will stop and listen and maybe even run like stink if we think we might have a problem, such as the occasional matrimonial tiff.

The original ideas behind the Centre's beginnings were to use the increasing interest that people seemed to be getting in birds of prey to get them to visit the Centre, and learn about the birds. At the same time we wanted to try to breed the birds in captivity and preferably, if possible, in front of the visitors. We also had to live, so the whole thing had to be a viable concern and support itself. I don't know, as they have never told me, but I am damn sure it did not support itself to start with, and my parents had to fund it until the time came that the Centre could stand on its own two feet. It barely does that even now.

These values behind the Centre have not changed a great deal. I am slightly less interested in the falconry aspects than my father. The side of the Centre that interests me most—and the side we have developed —is the breeding, conservation and education, although I thoroughly enjoy flying birds and hunting them. I have however, very little time these days, and flying birds for demonstration, for as long as I have,

Vultures, often thought of as unpleasant and ugly, can be very beautiful when seen at close quarters

has dulled the interest slightly. I am looking forward to a winter when all is complete here and I have nothing to do, then I will enjoy my falconry again. I think I may well be rather old at that point.

At first the Centre's plans for breeding raptors in captivity were laughed at by many people. Although zoos had occasionally bred birds of prey and so had some falconers and aviculturists, their success was rather more by accident than design (I am glad to say that this is no longer the case). To set out to keep a specialist collection of birds, nothing but birds of prey, to interest the public enough to pay to come and see them, and to breed from the birds was a pretty brave thing to do, particularly as none of us had much experience in either dealing with the public, coping with large numbers of birds, or trying to breed from them. Still, as can be seen today, the idea was not quite so far fetched. To date the Centre has bred more different species of birds of prey than any other single establishment, and many of those species have reared their young in front of the public. We have had hundreds of thousands of visitors over the years that we have been open, and most of them have left better informed about raptors than they were when they arrived. We have also learned a tremendous amount about birds of prey and about captive breeding in the intervening years.

Twenty years ago birds of prey were not viewed in as pleasant a light as they are today. Nowadays most gamekeepers no longer see them as so great a threat that they shoot everything that has a hooked beak, as was the case not so long ago. Fewer people are convinced that eagles kill sheep and steal babies out of prams; although how that idea came about I would love to know, as I can't think of anyone I know stupid enough to try and push a pram over the sort of terrain that eagles inhabit.

Raptors, however have always been thought of as red in tooth and claw and many people still envisage them with powers far greater than they actually have. Gentleness is not a trait usually applied to raptors and yet to watch an eagle or hawk feed its young is a wonderful sight. The care and patience these great birds have with their babies is fascinating to watch and this is what we want our visitors to experience, thus showing them a side of birds of prey which few people have the chance to see, and which puts the birds in a very different light.

We have always tried to fly the birds at demonstrations for all our visitors, only the weather or emergencies stopping us. The demonstrations have been one of the things which has made the Centre so popular and they have a very important educational value if done well. However I stress the 'done well' aspect. Numerous people now fly raptors for the public and, although many are very good, sadly there are others who do not always do the job well. I am always keen to point out that it is very much a demonstration rather than

Some of the working birds at The National Birds of Prey Centre

a display. All we attempt to do at the Centre is demonstrate either the different ways in which different species and family groups fly, or the training methods we use. It is not a circus act, nor should it ever be. The birds are only asked to do what comes naturally to them and this is very important. I suppose its equivalent would be a gundog demonstration, where much the same thing is happening. The dogs are behaving in the way that comes naturally to them. That natural talent is harnessed, and the training methods are shown.

Tremendously valuable work can be done with good demonstrations. I feel very strongly that I would much rather show my visitors trained birds, flying well and naturally, and if I have done my job well, in a spectacular fashion, under controllable circumstances, than I would see millions of people wandering around the countryside disturbing wildlife in an attempt to see birds of prey in the wild. So this is one of the main reasons for flying the birds here for our visitors. The birds are great public relations men (and women), and given the chance to be in front of visitors they manage to do most of our teaching work themselves! However, here at the Centre we do not allow visitors to handle or fly the birds. The reason for this is that I believe it is all too simple for people to think that the whole art of falconry is very easy. It is easy to hold a bird that someone

If done well, with the right commentary, flying demonstrations can be very educational

else has got tame, while they are standing by to help you, but it is a very far cry from training a bird from scratch and so I prefer to keep the birds a little removed from my visitors.

Having said that, we have from time to time had parties of blind children visit us here. This can be very exciting and, although extremely hard work, is very rewarding. In these cases we have a few birds that can be touched and handled by strangers, and we allow this handling of the calmer birds by the blind children. You have to have very steady birds though, as the children really do touch quite roughly to find out about them. We try to get the parties to visit at the right time of year for us to have baby birds available, so they can touch and feel the young. We also give them large eagle feathers to wave through the air to get the feel of the power of flight—within seconds the whole place is in chaos with feathers beating the air, waving up and down everywhere. We even fly birds for the children as they

Elmbridge Junior School
Elmbridge Road
Gloucester
6.11.86

Dear Mrs Parry-Jones,

   Thankyou for coming to our school with Astorix and Bramble. Mrs. Dinean said the slides were lovely. We all think that the way you trained Astorix was wonderful. Bramble was very well behaved. The slides were beautiful. Today we had a kite flying competition. The prizes were some bird gliders. One of them was a Peregrine.

   Thankyou once again,

love from

Rachel Coward,   Emma Cutting,   Jillian Hilditch,   Iane Kebbett,
Marc Fowler,   Matthew Callaghan, Danny
Lau,   matt hewslade, Janet Taylor,
Michele Gabrielle Cooper, Richard Smith,
Manesh Patel, Sarah Lodge, Nicola Holder,
Amanda Sweet,   Julie Martin,   Daniel Boucher,
Kate Whittard, Jenny Harwood, Warren Webb,
  Elizabeth Power, Matthew Gough, Charlotte
Ward, Richard Browett, Helen Jones, Robert
Ford,   Julie Rushmer, Ben Gamble,   Jaime Hosler,
Christopher   Hamer.

XXXXX

A letter from enthusiastic young visitors

can hear the bells and the noise of the birds' wings through the air. If we fly a falcon we know we can direct accurately, the children get very excited feeling the bird fly close over their heads.

All this is very much part of education, and education to us is one of the most interesting aspects of conservation, and probably the most important for the long-term future of birds of prey and all other species. If the right birds are used and the right message is put over to the audience, having a trained bird that will (hopefully) return to you, is a first class visual aid to an educational programme. The length of time that people remember the experience is amazing. I don't know about you, but I can't remember any of the lectures or outings we had at school. Come to think of it I do remember being coach sick somewhere in the New Forest, but that is by the by. We have visitors here who tell us how they remember my great uncle talking to them and flying a Golden Eagle at their school. They even remember the bird's name, Mr Ramshaw. This shows how much of an impact the experience of a live bird had on them. People who think that lectures with live birds will encourage falconry, and the illegal taking of birds, will be delighted to hear that not one of those visitors who have spoken to us and saw Mr Ramshaw, ever took up falconry.

Of course things don't always go quite as planned during flying demonstrations. In 1976 I managed to lose three birds in one summer. It was a particularly hot one, subsequently we learned how to fly birds in hot weather. I lost one of them at a show away from home, which would not have been quite so bad had I not been wearing medieval gear, and looked like a complete pratt. That in itself would have been okay if I had not been trudging through strange farmers' fields, slowly melting from the heat, and getting some very odd looks from those who saw me! At least if we have a bird go absent without leave at the Centre we can usually fly another one, but away from home I rely on my 'away team' and if things go wrong it can get embarrassing. It is not always my fault though. I have ended up in the ring swinging a lure to three microlight planes that were doing their demonstration above me, having started far too early. In the meantime my falcon was flying about half a mile away, wondering what the hell was going on. Several of my top falcons go a very long way up before returning, and can be out of sight for some time. I have to admit that I once spent twenty minutes swinging my lure to a seagull which I thought was my falcon—it did not come down to the lure.

We have our critics. Many falconers accuse us of being commercial because we are open to the public and sell some birds for falconry. I suppose they could be right, but what they probably don't realise is that if we were totally commercial we would not be open to the

A Lanner, flying well

public as this is very expensive. Most of our staff are here to cope with some aspect of dealing with visitors without whom we would only need to employ one person just to look after the birds, rather than up to twelve staff during the summer. The car park, paths, loos, etc etc have all been built solely for the public, as have play areas, seating, and numerous other facilities. We could, without doubt, make far more money with far fewer overheads by being closed to visitors and only breeding birds for sale. However we don't do that. I believe that as we have this collection of birds, we should share it with those people who visit us to enjoy seeing the birds as much as we do. Also we have a responsibility to pass on our experience and knowledge in order to assist both the birds in the wild and those in captivity. Falconry would be a lot poorer without people prepared to stand up for it, and not keep a 'low profile' hoping that all problems will go away.

We are also criticised by some bird societies who feel that we encourage falconry. Those societies don't approve of birds in captivity. I think that any harm we might do is far outweighed by the good, particularly on the educational side, and not forgetting that the number of species world wide now relying on captive populations to keep them from extinction is increasing every year. So, in spite of critics, the Centre has continued up to the present day and will continue, improving all the time.

When the first pens were built there were several constraints, finance being the main one (and still is to this very day); lack of experience being another. No one knew what sort of pens the birds would like. Now we have a far greater knowledge and are rebuilding all the time. Another problem we didn't understand was that you don't just build pens to keep the birds in, you build them to keep the public out. For example, there are very few fences, none we can afford to put up at the moment, that will stand being sat on, leant against, climbed over, walked along and subjected to any other abuse you can imagine (and some you can't).

Very tame birds can be a danger to themselves. I remember walking round the corner in the aviary area one day to find a man poking a stick, which he had broken off one of my shrubs, into the chest of a particularly tame Serpent Eagle, who was looking at him with the utmost disgust and disdain. I didn't say a word to him (surprisingly) but happened to be walking with a stick in my hand which I proceeded to poke into his chest—fairly gently, I hasten to add. He got the message immediately and nothing was said by either of us.

We often have tame young owls in what I call the baby pen. These will run up to people near the wire front and gently nibble fingers, but they are also very playful and somewhat destructive. One afternoon we heard a howl of misery from the baby pen, only to discover that a child had pushed a pound note through the wire at a baby eagle owl, who had quickly removed it from his fingers, dashed to the back of the pen with glee, and was proceeding to tear it into small and unusable pieces. I thought training a bird to do this might be quite a good way to fund raise, but we rescued the loot and returned it to its rightful owner, who promised to be more careful in future. We did not forget the owl, who was given a less expensive piece of paper to demolish.

Believe it or not, all this sort of thing, and the many other interesting and amusing happenings, are a valuable experience to the visitor. I am delighted to say that I think most leave the Centre having had an enjoyable day, learnt something without feeling lectured at and having a better impression of birds of prey. Few will forget the experience of having a bird fly close to them and many will treasure it for the rest of their lives, and this is the whole point of The National Birds of Prey Centre.

Falconry as a career!

One thing I would like to say early on in this book, please think hard before you decide you want to take up falconry as a career. There are no careers in falconry. There are a few jobs available in things like clearing rubbish dumps with falcons, but this is generally unsuccessful, as is clearing airfields, unless it is done properly, using the right birds for the job. One of my staff actually worked on rubbish tip clearance and seemed to spend all his time hitting tin lids with sticks to frighten the crows and gulls away—hardly falconry. Very few people employ someone to be their falconer; I know of only two in this country. Most people interested in falconry do all the training and flying of their birds themselves.

We have many letters each year from people who have visited the Centre, seen similar establishments, or watched us on the television. They ask for jobs because they are interested in falconry or birds of prey. The job we do here is *not* falconry. In fact, we probably have far less time with the birds than most falconers who are just flying their own birds as a hobby. The only time we have to handle the

birds is during the demonstrations, and, as already mentioned, even that palls after a while.

All my staff will tell you that I am so mean, I don't give them enough time to hunt birds properly, especially during the winter months, when all available daylight hours are used in building, care and maintenance. Most of the time we are either mowing lawns, cleaning loos (great job that one!) raking compartments, cleaning up bird droppings from night or sick quarters, or dealing with the visitors. None of which is tremendous fun after a while, and none of which really relates to falconry. If you are interested in taking up falconry, then for heaven's sake sort yourself out with a job that gives you plenty of daylight hours, and take it as a serious hobby. You will enjoy it far more, as everyone here can tell you from great experience. And don't think that places like this are going to teach you falconry with you working for them on a volunteer basis for nothing, because very few places have the time, and they may be running falconry courses commercially in which case you can hardly expect to be taught for nothing.

The National Birds of Prey Centre has one of the largest collections of birds of prey in the world and we hope to increase it slowly as we go along. Each species we succeed with means that if it needs help in the future we are already, by sharing our hard learned knowledge, a long way along the road to assisting it. Each species that we can teach visitors about is a little extra knowledge disseminated, all of which helps in the long run.

Tawny Eagle

2 BIRDS USED IN FALCONRY

We sell some of our captive-bred birds to falconers. I usually ask them to let us know how the birds get on, as we get attached to birds we breed and like to hear how they do. I enjoy it when they do well and when I hear from some very pleased new owners. I had a phone call from a chap who bought a female Harris Hawk from us two years ago. He has phoned occasionally, but this time he was pretty cheerful to say the least. He had in the last two weeks caught two ducks, one in mid-air with a good lead on the Harris who was on the ground, one guinea fowl and a squirrel. I too was delighted, not because things were finally coming together for him and the bird, but because he had persevered. I will risk boring everyone by repeating throughout this book the necessity of perseverance with training, flying and breeding birds. Two and a half years is the minimum that should be given to any flying bird before it will really develop, and much longer for breeding birds.

I hate to hear about people who go through bird after bird, never persevering or giving the birds a chance, always blaming the bird for being useless. I know which out of the falconer and the bird I consider to be useless. The thing that makes me so cross is that the poor birds that these people continually get rid of, go from one person to another, slowly getting worse and worse manners until no one wants them. So, give all birds time.

One of the important factors in falconry is to match the right bird to the right person. The aspects to take into account are the flying areas, time available for flying, quarry available, and the temperament of the person involved. There is no point in a temperamental person getting a temperamental bird as they will never get on. A knowledge of the different species, what they are like and what they are capable of, both in captivity and in the wild, is vital.

With far greater import controls both here and abroad, and recent changes in the Convention for the International Trade in Endangered Species (CITES), the species of birds that are reasonably available to falconers have now decreased again. Although there may be the odd unusual bird, pre-import controls, still around, such as a very few of the Asian Hawk Eagles, most of these are very old. The chances of these species and many others ever being available to falconry again are almost nil. Therefore I am going to discuss the birds that are generally used and which should be available in reasonable numbers for many years to come, and some that are not suitable for falconry, but might be thought so. As most of us live in areas more suited to the hawk and buzzard families, these birds are now tending to be the most desired. Generally, the buzzard family is the most suited to beginners.

Buzzards

Not all buzzards are of use to falconers. The Swainson's Buzzard and the Rough-legged Buzzard for example are quite large birds but they seem to be of much less use than the Common Buzzard. The Honey Buzzard is not even a buzzard and for falconry is quite useless besides being difficult to look after. The three buzzards that are liable to be used in Britain are the native Common Buzzard and the two non-indigenous species, the Redtailed Buzzard and the Ferruginous Buzzard. The Americans call these Redtailed and Ferruginous Hawks but don't be misled, they are true *buteos*. The first two species are suitable for the more enclosed country that most of us have available, whereas the Ferruginous is an open-country bird.

The reason that some of us consider buzzards the best beginner's birds is mainly their size and robustness. Small birds such as Sparrowhawks and Kestrels, although they are probably less frightening than having a large bird such as a buzzard to deal with, are very, very easy to kill should the beginner make any mistakes. Buzzards being larger have more body reserves to survive being cut down too low in weight. Their larger body will also withstand more handling than the little birds. I suppose another reason why I like the buzzard as a beginner's bird, is that if you have the courage to face an untrained buzzard that is footing and biting you, then perhaps you will be a reasonable falconer. If you are worried by their size don't consider even starting.

Buzzards, like eagles, are bright birds and will find the easiest way of making a living, both in the wild state and the trained. I don't think lazy is the word to describe either family group, opportunist would be better. This however, is the reason that buzzards are labelled lazy and not particularly good for falconry. Most eagles and

buzzards in the wild will take the easier way out, living on smallish quarry and preferably carrion if they can find it. But in the breeding season when they have young to feed, watch and see how they will take larger quarry to feed and sustain their young.

None of the buzzard family including Redtails, Ferruginous and the buzzard-like Harris Hawk is easy to enter to quarry. Only the true hawks seem to catch quarry despite what mistakes falconers make in the early stages. I will definitely agree that Common Buzzards are difficult to enter, but I will not agree that they will not catch quarry *if* the falconer perseveres and gives the bird every opportunity of (a) getting to peak fitness—as the quarry will undoubtedly be—and (b) finding enough quarry for the bird to fly at. Unless you have done this for at least two and a half years, preferably more, you cannot say that you have given that bird a fair crack of the whip.

One thing I would say to beginners who have looked at the subject thoroughly, and know that they seriously want to fly a bird for the forseeable future. That is, don't necessarily think in terms of buying a beginner's bird, before moving on to other birds. If you can afford it, buy a Harris or a Redtail to start with, and as you improve the bird will improve with you. There are three reasons I say this. The first is that I worry a little about all the buzzards that have taught beginners, and are then no longer wanted. If you buy the bird that will suit you right the way through, this problem does not arise. The second reason is that you are going to spend a great deal of time getting a bird good, and you might as well do it with a suitable bird that you will want to fly for years to come. Both Harrises and Redtails make good beginner's birds and will fly for you for up to twenty years getting better each season. This is cheap yearly hunting if you divide the buying price by twenty. The third reason is that the price of the bird you eventually want may well go up, making it difficult for many people to afford to continue.

COMMON BUZZARD (*Buteo buteo*)

In my opinion this is a maligned bird. The older falconers, who never had to learn on buzzards because other birds were very easily obtained, tend to be very rude about it. There are also many younger falconers who will tell you that the Common Buzzard is useless and cannot catch anything; they are wrong. It can without doubt catch rabbits and it does so in the wild, although it is probably fair to say that a male will be hard pushed to hold a decent sized full grown rabbit. It is reasonable to say that what a bird can catch in the wild state, it can catch when trained. In fact, with the assistance of man,

Common Buzzard

many trained birds of prey are taking quarry that they would not normally tackle in the wild.

The temperament of the Common Buzzard is good and fairly steady which suits most beginners, and they are quite difficult to lose as they do not travel great distances in flight. They, like most of the buzzards, will, in the early stages of training, snatch at your hands with their feet, as well as bite you. So be careful with your hands, just because they have reasonably small feet doesn't mean they can't hurt—ask a rabbit. If you persevere with a Common Buzzard you should be able to take rabbits, moorhens and squirrels; some falconers have taken the odd small hare and pheasant.

Common Buzzards are *very* difficult to sex. Their size varies so much that weighing the bird will tell you almost nothing, apart from its weight. The only sure way is to have them surgically sexed until sexing can be done with a sample of living tissue, at which

Susie, a Redtailed Buzzard

time surgical sexing will become unnecessary. However, if you are happy with your bird, why worry what sex it is, unless you want to put it into a breeding project (at which point it becomes rather more important!).

REDTAILED BUZZARD (*Buteo jamaicensis*)

These birds are a good deal bigger than our Common Buzzard, and they are excellent for many falconers. They have a good temperament as long as they have not been imprinted (see page 96) in any way; if they have, they can be dangerous. They are more than capable of taking rabbits, pheasants, moorhens, coots and squirrels. The females will take hares regularly, if you give them the chance to learn about taking quarry by the head. Don't expect any bird to take hares immediately. As an average hare weighs about 6lb (2.7kg) and they can go a good deal heavier, give the bird the chance to learn.

I am afraid that I don't agree with my Father when he says that Redtails won't take feathered game in fair flight. They can and will if they are fit enough. But pheasants are fast and it needs a bird that is confident in itself and in its fitness to persist.

Redtails come from a very wide area and so vary greatly in size and colour, depending on the range from which the original birds came. Colour means nothing to the capabilities of hunting, and size will only mean that if they are on the small side they may not be able to hold a hare, but they will be fine for all other normal quarry. As with the Common Buzzard they are not too easy to lose as long as you don't let them start to self hunt. As they are a more successful hunter than a Common Buzzard because of their greater foot size, they will take to the wild state quicker.

FERRUGINOUS BUZZARD (*Buteo regalis*)

These birds are very different from the other two species of buzzard mentioned. They have long pointed wings that are very falcon-like in shape, and the feathers are much stiffer than other buzzards'. They have a huge gape (mouth) which means that they can eat their kills very quickly. The feet are small in comparison to the body size, but very powerful, especially in the females, who are bigger than redtails. Sexing them is very easy as the size difference is great.

They are not good beginner's birds as they have a difficult and nervous temperament. One day they behave well and the next they seem almost untrained. Nor are they birds suited to enclosed or wooded country. One problem is that if they do kill at any distance from the falconer, and this is often the case, they will probably have gorged themselves before he or she can get there and remove the kill. So you may only get one kill per day. Another problem I have come across is that no amount of coaxing will get them to fly back to you

Colorado, a Ferruginous Buzzard

downwind on a windy day. This habit disappears when the bird gets fit, and more confident on the wing, but I always had to walk round to the upwind side to call in Colorado, my female, then she was very obedient.

Ferruginous come from the open plains in the United States and Canada and need similar space to reach any potential in this country. They appear clumsy in areas that are too enclosed for them. Flown in open hilly country they are ideal. They will hill soar and can stay up on windy days for long periods.

They need enormous patience to be got going well and if you don't have it, don't take one on, it is not fair on the bird. Those people who have persisted and have flown Ferruginous in the right places have had tremendous fun, and the length of slip these birds will take on is amazing. Given the space and the time there is little that the females are not capable of taking. The males being considerably smaller will not manage hares. They are very difficult to enter and to start with may well be frightened by a dead or dummy rabbit. This is mainly due to the fact that most captive-bred birds are fed on day-old chicks and never see a rabbit until they are faced with it during training. Is it then surprising that many birds are frightened when asked to catch and eat something other than the food they have seen for all of their short lives? Once they learn that rabbits are good grub they will get the idea if only you—guess what—persevere!

I think the Ferruginous is a beautiful bird with great potential in open country, but it is not for those of us with lack of time or space.

HARRIS HAWK (*Parabuteo unicinctus*)
This is one of the most interesting birds there is to fly because of its ability and brains. These birds really start to show excellent form as they get older and more experienced, and benefit from plenty of time given to them. Once over the initial training period they are very tame birds and a delight to handle, although don't think of them as a pushover. We have a couple of males that have frightened our students greatly on falconry courses by not feeding for ten days and getting dangerously thin.

Their tameness has led some falconers to think that the birds are not good hunters, as they will be obedient to the fist at a far higher weight than that which they need to be to put any effort into hunting, at least in the early stages. I like to fly all my birds at as high a weight as possible, but young Harrises need to be a little hungry before they will really get going. Once they have learnt what hunting is all about, they can be flown in very high condition.

Harrises will happily fly together in groups, and pairs will help one another in hunting, both in the trained state and in the wild. First clutches of young will even help parents feed second clutches.

This makes them very sociable falconer's birds, both birdwise and falconerwise. Some people both in this country and the United States go out in groups, each member flying a Harris, letting the birds hunt together. I don't think this will get the best out of individual birds, but occasionally it won't hurt as long as the land and the quarry are treated with respect. It can be a good idea to fly potential and proved pairs together after the breeding season to keep or build the pair bond.

They are powerful birds and there is, as in the Ferruginous, a great difference in the size of the sexes. I have heard some falconers say that they cannot catch rabbits with the males. I am afraid I consider that to be rubbish. All the males we have flown here have taken and held full-grown buck rabbits weighing $4\frac{1}{2}$lb (2kg) on a regular basis. A good friend of mine who has a male Harris on loan from us has just taken his first hare and expects to catch more. Although this is not what I would expect a male Harris to be able to tackle with ease, there is something wrong with either the bird or the falconer if males are not catching rabbits, and I suspect the latter.

Without doubt the best Harris I have seen flown is my father's female, Islay. This bird is taking 6–7lb (3kg) hill hares by the score. I saw her chase four hares up-hill one afternoon, gaining on them the whole time before being beaten to the top, the fifth threw her off so violently that most birds would have given up, she then took and killed the sixth in fine style. She only missed the seventh because it found the wreck of an old car to hide in. All that takes fitness and courage both of which she has plenty, because she is flown almost every day, apart from the breeding season, and was not over-faced to start with.

They do have some disadvantages although I like them for it. They are very bright. We find that we can't let ours loose too close to home or they will fly back without us. You cannot hide a kill in order to pick it up on the way home, at least not if the Harris sees you do it. They will fly back to where you hid it and pull it out. They are also very playful and will at times infuriate you—you may have just had the perfect flush of a really good pheasant, only to see the Harris Hawk far too busy killing a branch to have seen the flush anyway. Generally they don't like dogs, probably because one of the few enemies they have in the wild is the coyote.

Harrises have become known as the weekend falconer's bird. This in some ways is a shame, as a weekend bird will never really be fit, and so will rarely show the sort of style and success rate that a fit bird will have. I don't really think that you should have falconry as a sport if you can only fly birds at the weekend. After all, there is no way you could keep a horse stabled, or a dog shut up, and only

Cathy, an adult Harris Hawk

exercise it two days a week, but that is what many people expect to be able to do with their birds. However they are very useful to falconers with a limited amount of time for manning (handling and taming rather than training and flying) as, once tame, they will generally stay that way with very little manning time spent on them, unlike the true hawks who need constant manning.

One only has to look at the feet of a Harris Hawk to see why it is such a good bird. Feet are what count in a bird of prey. Its body size is not really that significant. Red Kites have a larger body than a Harris Hawk and look huge in the air, but their feet are tiny in comparison to that body. Our Blyth's Hawk Eagles were far smaller than a Red Kite with very large and powerful feet, thus making them a very useful bird for falconry unlike the Red Kite.

When training young Harris Hawks you have to be very careful not to start too early. These are intelligent birds and can, if removed from their parents as soon as they are hard down, and immediately cut down in weight, imprint onto the handler and start to scream. So if you buy yourself a young Harris don't cut it down straight away. Put it into a pen and give it at least a couple of weeks to settle before starting to take its weight down. If you have not got a pen available for the bird, in my opinion you should not get the bird in the first place.

Hawks

The hawks are the sprinters of the bird world and their initial burst of speed is great. If they are not fit they will not be able to hold that speed for long. They need to be got fit just as much as any other bird, but unlike the buzzards they are easy to enter onto quarry, as they only ever think of chasing things. They are very nervous and need to be got used to strange things such as tractors, dogs, people, farm animals, bicycles, motor vehicles and so on ad infinitum.

None of the true hawks are suitable as beginner's birds. Nor are they suitable for people with unpredictable lives or lack of time. There are two species of hawk available in this country, the Goshawk and Sparrowhawk, with two others that may be available in small numbers in the future, the Cooper's Hawk and Black Sparrowhawk. One very often reads how hawks (*accipiters*) are subject to fits—for reasons unknown—rubbish. The main reason hawks have fits is because they are difficult to train and handle, so falconers used too often cut their weight down hard to get them tractable. They left them at this weight regardless of the work the bird was doing and regardless of the weather. The poor birds were in such low condition that they got all sorts of deficiencies and ended up having fits. There is absolutely NO reason why a falconer's bird should have these, and in this more knowledgeable time it is unforgivable for a falconer's bird to die of them. If you don't have the time to get a hawk really tame, so that you are flying it through training and confidence rather than through starvation, then for heaven's sake (and the bird's) don't have one.

GOSHAWK (*Accipiter gentilis*)

Sadly for all of us this bird is very difficult to obtain at the moment. Because of this it is also one of the most expensive to buy. If you don't have the use of a good telemetry set, take my advice and don't spend a fortune on a Goshawk. They are incredibly easy to lose, and you would do better to stick to a Harris Hawk, which will fly nearly as well and is less likely to bugger off at the drop of a hat. If I had the time to fly one well, this is the only bird I would bother to insure against loss—if I could get cover for it.

Goshawks are a hunting machine and I am not really convinced that they actually have brains. They, like the Peregrine, only have one speed and that is flat out. Correction, they have one other speed, sitting still, often in an inaccessible tree for several hours at a time.

Called the 'cook's bird' in the Middle Ages, they are happy to tackle both fur and feather although the males are unlikely to hold a full grown hare without swift assistance. Very temperamental and needing handling and manning every day, they need a falconer with lots of time and patience. As with other hawks anything that can upset a Goshawk, will.

If you do have the time, patience and good hunting ground, then they are very exciting birds to fly, with little or no fear.

SPARROWHAWK (*Accipiter nisus*)

There are lots of different species of sparrowhawk all over the world, the largest being the Black Sparrowhawk from Africa. They are all finely built birds, much more physically delicate than the more robust Goshawk and Cooper's Hawk. All of what I would call the true Sparrowhawks, as opposed to the Goshawks, are bird catchers. Their long fine legs and feet are ideal to grab birds from the air, or anywhere else come to that. This fineness makes them even more difficult to handle than the Goshawk, and it is very easy to damage their talons.

The European Sparrowhawk has as nervous a temperament as the Goshawk, but as it is far smaller it is infinitely more difficult to train and to maintain. A quarter of an ounce can be the difference between a healthy bird and a very sick one. If you are flying it close to the margin in weight, you can actually watch the bird go underweight while being flown. I really don't think 99 per cent of falconers should even attempt a male (musket) Sparrowhawk as they are just

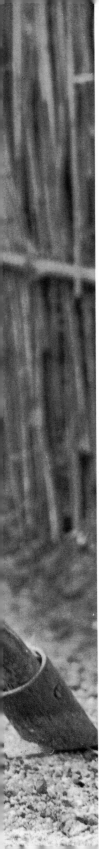

Sparrowhawk

Immature male Goshawk

too small. Half an hour late with their food can be a matter of life or death in very cold weather.

Sparrowhawks are probably the only bird, except for owls, that can benefit from handling as a baby. If you take a Sparrowhawk at about two weeks and hand rear it from then, it will imprint on you and consequently be far tamer and thus can be flown at a higher weight. The handling must be consistent though. If you don't keep it up the bird will revert to being wild just like any other spar. The odd thing is that these are the only birds apart from some owls that can be hand reared and may well still breed naturally. Female Goshawks on the other hand are even more likely to kill the males if they are imprinted even to a small degree.

The best thing about a Sparrowhawk is that you don't need vast areas of land to be able to have a great deal of fun hunting. I used to fly mine (she was called Benjamin's Daughter) just in the local fields or around the local farm buildings. I probably had more fun with that bird than any other because quarry is so easy to find.

They are the last bird a beginner should contemplate and should only be flown by very experienced falconers.

COOPER'S HAWK (*Accipiter cooperii*)

I hope these excellent birds may become more available in Britain. They have been flown here in the past. We are trying to build up breeding pairs as I think they would be a useful addition to the species of hawks flown in this country. They are very like a small version of our Goshawk, but bigger than our Sparrowhawk. Obviously the quarry they will take is smaller, but the females will take three-quarter grown rabbits and should be able to hold hen pheasants. The American falconers have great fun flying them at quail. So a really fit female should be able to take partridge. The males will take starling and probably magpies, if you can give them the opportunity. No one has bred Cooper's Hawks in this country to date and few Americans bother, as they can take them legally from the wild in enough numbers to make captive breeding unnecessary.

BLACK SPARROWHAWK (*Accipiter melanoleucus*)

Bigger than a Cooper's Hawk but finer built, these are very difficult birds to manage. I think one of the reasons is that they normally live in a very hot country where none of the wildlife moves much between 9am and 4pm. The falconers in Africa take their birds out and fly them usually in the evenings. This suits the birds well. Over here the weather is rarely hot and so these birds seem to have an excess of energy, and spend most of their time bating. They are as temperamental as all the Sparrowhawks and very difficult to man. Like the European Sparrowhawk they have fine skin and are

Diana, adult female Cooper's Hawk

susceptible to bumblefoot if great care is not taken. Of the birds we have bred and that I have let leave the Centre, one male was dead within two weeks and the females have generally caused many problems to their new owners. They are only any use at feathered quarry as they are not robust enough for rabbits and the like. The thickness of leg on our males is only that of a pencil's, not even as thick as a female Cooper's Hawk. Although we breed them here at the Centre, they are only suitable for pretty dedicated falconers, with plenty of feathered game and plenty of time and patience.

Falcons

Falcons, as most people will know, need open countryside to hunt successfully. I think sometimes there is confusion as to what open country is. Moorland; downland with no woods, scrub or barbed-wire fences, and some of the huge open fields in the east side of England, all these could be described as open country. If there are areas of cover near where you intend flying a falcon the quarry will make for it every time, and this will make hunting with falcons much more difficult. With too much cover the falcon will eventually give up chasing through lack of success. Both Merlins and Peregrines therefore need open space to be flown successfully. Some of the foreign species can work in slightly more enclosed spaces, but you are unlikely to get very high stoops, as they would not be effective where there is cover. I have not flown falcons at game, I don't have the time or the land. It does not interest me to rush up to Scotland for just two weeks, as this never gives the birds enough time to get proficient, and I certainly don't have six weeks to spare. So I won't tell you how to hunt with longwings; that would be ridiculous. However, I have flown most of the longwings for many years here at the Centre for demonstration work. One can learn a great deal about the different species with as long and consistent an association as we have had with them here.

There are a number of people who, having been influenced by watching flying demonstrations, just fly falcons to the lure for pleasure. I can't really knock it, but one thing I would warn about. Flying one falcon every day to the lure is very different from doing what we do here. Each of us flies several demonstration falcons. There is always the stimulus of trying to get your birds better than anyone else's birds, and of flying falcons in front of an interested audience. Just flying the same falcon every day, year in year out without much stimulus gets boring, and I write with experience, have actually done it for a year and a half. It is less interesting than taking a dog for a

Black Sparrowhawk

walk, as little will change over the years. So before trying it, think if you really want to fly a bird to the lure for the next fifteen to twenty years of its life.

Although I am about to write about the different species and probably compare some aspects of one with another, please remember that such comparison is a great mistake. They are all very different and all have their own merits. Many species in the same genus are suited to totally different ways of training and flying. One does not have the right to judge unless one has flown a number of one species consistently.

LANNER (*Falco biarmicus*)
Of all the falcons, this is probably my favourite, mainly due to the numbers of Lanners I have flown and the innumerable times they have flown their best and not let me down. As a demonstration bird they are consistently the best.

They seem to divide into two groups. First, the shorter, more compact and peregrine-shaped ones such as a falcon we have here called Blewitt, who is well known. These types fly with fast wing beats and stoop hard. Blewitt will soar in the right weather and goes up out of sight. When he does decide to return, he just folds, and many of us have seen him give breathtaking stoops. The other kind seem to be lighter built, longer in the wing and tail, and are more butterfly-like in flight, more inclined to save energy and soar or float. Fern, my other excellent falcon, was more of this type and although female, she and Blewitt flew at the same weight. These more buoyant Lanners are much more manoeuvrable. The four most exciting stoops I have ever seen, and that includes all the falcons flown at quarry in various parts of the world, have all been made by Fern who folds, like Blewitt, but sometimes waited until she was directly above me, totally vertical, and then drop, twisting on the way down. Twice she has had me in tears through the sheer joy of it.

Lanners have a lovely temperament and are a pleasure to handle. As a hunting bird I don't think they have really been done justice. A captive-bred Lanner introduced to partridges would be first class. I have seen them take francolin in Zimbabwe in good style and see no reason why they shouldn't be just as successful over here. I think the reason they have not done as well as they might, is that the falconers who suffer from Terminal Peregrinitus have never really given them a chance, considering that anything that is not a Peregrine is bound to be inferior. Those falconers who have flown them in the past have not been quite as experienced in flying longwings as they might have been, usually flying Lanners because they could not get hold of

Immature Lanner

Lanners are very manoeuvrable and can be just as dramatic as Peregrines (yes – it *is* the right way up!). Precious, an immature Lanner

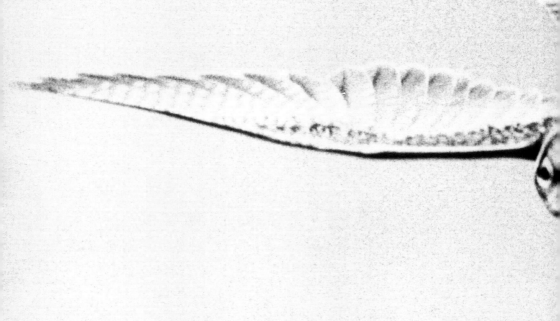

Jan, an adult Lugger

Peregrines. In my experience, flying imported passage or adult birds was never very successful in any sphere, they had already learnt all sorts of bad and lazy habits. Flying eyass, captive-bred birds should have made these a much more successful hunting bird.

You may have noticed that I have not put any weights down for birds. This it because there is nothing more dangerous than average weights, particularly for beginners to the sport. Lanners are a good example. We have flown males weighing from 14oz to 1lb 6oz (.4 to .6kg) flying weight, and females from 1lb 3oz to 1lb 10oz (.5 to .7kg). So you can see how dangerous it would be if a beginner tried to fly a large male at 14oz. It would be very dead at that weight.

LUGGER FALCON (*Falco lugger*)

This bird has now gone onto the Red List, which means that it is an endangered species in the wild. These are very different birds in temperament from the Lanners. They are much more difficult to tame and to handle, being prone to throwing tantrums and screaming in fury.

My staff all dislike Luggers, but that is because they have never experienced a good parent-reared youngster. Unfortunately far fewer Luggers are bred than Lanners and many of these are hand reared, which spoils them. I have to admit that although I like Luggers a great deal, it is about the last bird I would accept if it had been hand reared. Not that I accept hand-reared birds anyway. We have had four Luggers here that were first-class flyers and two of them frequently caught quarry as well. They think about what they are doing and all the females we flew made light of even the strongest winds. They are not the falcon for someone starting out on longwings for the first time.

Both Lanners and Luggers tend to make their leashes absolutely disgusting. They are difficult to keep in really tip-top condition feather-wise as they will often roost on the ground rather than on their blocks. They benefit greatly from being kept loose in a pen once they are tame and trained.

I don't agree that Luggers are inferior birds to Lanners. They are just very different. The Luggers we have flown have tended to be more aggressive than the Lanners and again I feel very strongly that the eyass bird flown in the right place, at the right quarry, by experienced or persevering people, would be a successful falconry bird.

PRAIRIE FALCON (*Falco mexicanus*)

Prairies are very under-rated birds in this country. They are tremendously courageous and would make an excellent alternative to the Peregrine. They can also cope with slightly more enclosed country. All the eyass captive-bred birds we have flown at the Centre have gained height naturally and very early on in their flying lives.

They are incredibly greedy, as indeed are my Sakers. The first ones we handled seemed to have an awful temperament—worse than the worst Lugger. But I think having trained several more since then, that it was because they were slightly imprinted. I did know of one Prairie falcon in the United States that would lie up her owner's arm to bite it above the glove! My own breeding male Prairie, Taco, was pretty temperamental and difficult to handle. He had to be grounded from demonstration work because of incessantly chasing anything that moved. I will never forget one day when a Kestrel in a pen behind the Hawk Walk decided to get out via Taco; we heard this dreadful noise from his compartment. It took three of us to hold him down and extricate a very surprised Kestrel, luckily none the worse for wear. I thought I would have to leave Taco for at least twenty-four hours to recover from being manhandled, but not a bit of it. He shook himself and leaped back to the hole the Kestrel had made, looking for the next bird to appear!

Prairies seem to range quite far from the falconer very early on, but are pretty obedient. They are also very persistent. Taco thought nothing of stooping straight into thick cover after quarry, forcing his way through and appearing on the other side still looking for the game and still following it, if it was in sight. Our males are fairly small but the females are enormous. There is a greater size difference between

Socrates, an immature male Prairie Falcon

Iraq, an immature male Saker

the sexes than with Lanners and Luggers, although this could just be the offspring from my own pair.

Prairies are great birds, although not for the inexperienced and not for the nervous. You have to have good nerves to cope with them and plenty of time to get them really tame. One note of warning; they tend to be very aggressive in breeding pens. We have given up trying to manipulate eggs with our pair. We had too many broken by the defending female. We just leave them to it and they hatch and rear their own young with no assistance. You can always tell the day the young Prairies have been ringed, as at least two of us will come in for coffee bleeding profusely.

SAKER (*Falco cherrug*)

The second largest of all the falcons and, at the risk of sounding repetitious, these birds have not been well understood in this country, for the same reasons as many of the other imported falcons, they already had habits that were difficult to break. Training eyasses is so much more pleasant than passage or haggard birds, because you have a clean page to write on. One of the problems with the imported birds was that they had a little, rather disconcerting, habit of migrating while being flown. I always found this quite funny, although I don't suppose those to whom it has happened did. The thought of the bird disappearing off on migration without even a backward glance to the falconer, to be spotted next somewhere in Europe or Asia, definitely tickled my sense of humour. So far none of our captive-bred birds has migrated—the laugh will be on me if they do—although I would wish them the best of luck on the trip.

Of all the falcons available in this country, with the exception of New Zealand Falcons, Sakers are the most versatile. They seem to prefer ground game and, if you are not too much of a purist, they would easily take rabbits and pheasants if given enough open ground to reach full speed. I like their temperament, their greed means that you can fly them at a nice high weight (but be very careful not to get them too high) and they train very easily, with only one hiccup—it is sometimes difficult to get them to catch the lure in mid air for the first few attempts. This is, I think, because they prefer ground kills. However, once they get the idea it is not a problem.

The females are big birds and therefore tend to be clumsy to start with. They need to be given time and patience before they become proficient and fit. The males are easier to get fit and agile because they are smaller. Like the Prairies, all mine have gained reasonable height fairly quickly, except for one—he thinks he is a lawn-mower and cuts the grass all the time, flying at approximately 6 inches (15 cm)

Cade, an adult male Peregrine

off the ground. Still, he surprised me and the local rooks yesterday by chasing them quite persistently and at a height considerably greater than 6 inches, so he will improve given time.

Don't cut them down in weight too hard or they can scream, as can Prairies, and it seems to make no difference that they have been totally parent-hatched and reared in a solid walled pen. They are greedy and food matters to them. Cut them down hard too early and you will get them screaming. That could be said of any birds, come to think of it.

PEREGRINE (*Falco peregrinus peregrinus*)

There is probably more rubbish written about this bird than any other. I am glad to say that the stories about its potential speed have now been reduced by some 200mph, and so it would at least have the chance of coming through a stoop with all its feathers still in place, rather than bald; 120–130 is all I reckon they do.

Often called the king of falconry birds, it is in fact of less use to most of us in Britain than any other with the exception of the Kestrel. To fly them in anything other than true open country is probably a waste of time and, although telemetry should make finding them easier, you will certainly spend plenty of time looking for them if flying them in country with cover.

Peregrines are the second fastest of the falcons with a higher wing loading than most others of the genus. They have shorter wings and tails in comparison to the other falcons and thus they lack manoeuvrability. Their temperament is good and they are pretty easy to train. We have tried flying many of our young Peregrines here for demonstration and always had to give up. They invariably ended up chasing quarry and kept disappearing, with us in hot pursuit.

To do justice to a Peregrine in Britain you should really have up to six weeks holiday (more is even better), access to a good grouse moor and a first class dog to point and flush the game. This is an expensive hobby and few of us can afford it. Peregrines can be flown out of the hood at rooks, but again open land is needed. Tiercels can be flown at partridges if they are available.

GYR FALCON (*Falco rusticolus*)

I have just got one as a gift—I'll tell you more about it in the next book.

Gyrs are the largest of the falcons and undoubtedly the fastest. Several of my American friends fly them, and a few breed them. They live in the open tundras and need similar space over here to be able to perform in the way they are capable of. Until they are over here

An immature Gyr Falcon (grey phase)

in reasonable numbers and are being bred regularly, which is very difficult I am told, they are prohibitively expensive—too expensive for most of us to risk flying them free even if we had them.

Gyrs are absolutely stunning birds to look at. One time I had one of them on my fist it bated and all the papers in the room disappeared out of the window and the gas fire blew out! They are immensely powerful and look just like a beautiful statue.

There are several subspecies, and they come in three colours normally; one almost black, the more usual grey phase, and the much desired white. I admit to wanting to try to breed and fly them very much indeed.

MERLIN (*Falco columbarius*)
Although these lovely little falcons are the quickest to train and have flying free, they are definitely not beginner's birds as they are very small and quite delicate. The old falconers used to fly them just for one season and then release them. This was partly because Merlins are rarely ever as spectacular in flight after their first season and partly because they were difficult to bring through the winter alive. Nowadays we know a great deal more and should be well able to keep Merlins for years. They are difficult birds to keep. They are prone to coccidiosis which although it doesn't normally kill them, can become a killer if it flares up when the birds are put under stress, such as a change of owner. They also tend to get bumblefoot easily. If flown at larks, which is the traditional quarry, don't forget that you will need a quarry licence from the DoE.

Hybrid Falcons (*Falco?*)

The main thing to remember with any cross breeding is that although you can blend the best of two species you can also blend the worst. I haven't had a great deal of experience with hybrids. The Americans have a great deal more knowledge than I, as they started the whole thing. Some falcons will hybridise naturally, ie they will produce fertile eggs if paired without having the alternative of the right species as a mate. In these cases the breeder does not have to resort to artificial insemination. It is said that the Saker and the Gyr will interbreed in the wild, where their ranges cross.

We were given two hybrid Lanner/Luggers. They were absolutely awful birds but, to be fair, they had been hand reared for too long so it was not really fair to judge them. I don't think Lanner/Lugger is a particularly useful cross. If crosses are to be made, make one that will be useful. I strongly disapprove of silly crosses such as Peregrine/ Kestrel or, worse, Gyr/American Kestrel. I also think we may be making a rod for our own backs at a later date. The anti-falconry brigade may use these hybrid crosses as a reason to try and ban the use of non-indigenous species, although with no good reason in my opinion.

There can be no doubt about the vigour of some of these birds. Martin Jones, in collaboration with the NBoPC produces Saker/Peregrines last year (1987) and the offspring are dynamite – good looking, nice tempered, powerful and very interested in chasing any decent sized bird in the neighbourhood. This was much to the disgust of one member of our staff, who was left holding a large and heavy panel while the others on the building team disappeared to watch one of the male hybrids just miss its first crow.

I have now flown four in the last five years and can't praise them highly enough.

Eagles

There are only a few species of eagle flown in this country. There are also very few people who should even attempt flying them. The flying of all eagles will quickly be banned if irresponsible people try to fly them in the wrong areas. I don't believe that eagles should be flown and hunted anywhere other than unpopulated areas of very open countryside. The only eagles that can cope with enclosed hunting areas are the hawk eagles.

Almost all eagles are capable of killing small dogs, my terrier has been grabbed by two of our eagles and the two Goldens are convinced that he is a rather peculiar rabbit. You can just imagine headlines in a newspaper if a dog ever gets killed in front of its owner while he is taking it for a walk, or worse still, someone wearing a coat with a fur collar gets grabbed and hurt by an eagle. This *could* happen if eagles are flown in populated areas where people walk. There are very few places in the south of England where you can guarantee not to bump into walkers. Even the Yorkshire moors are well walked over these days. Unless all of us are responsible with these large birds, falconry with eagles will end up banned and eagles will be put onto the dangerous animals list. Eagles have been flown by responsible falconers for centuries and none of the general public has been either hurt or worried by them. Let us strive to keep it that way.

Many eagles will test the handler, finding how much they can get away with in terms of behaviour. They will needle a new handler to see what he will put up with. We have found here at the Centre that often they take badly to being handled by more than one person. Of all the birds of prey they benefit more from a one person relationship.

(*overleaf*) Martial Eagle (not suitable for falconry in the UK or anywhere else unless you are insane!)

They are very powerful and the large ones can be very heavy to carry, so the handler will also have to be fit. It is better never to take food from an eagle—at times it can be impossible! We fly all ours to small pieces of meat, and to start with we do not teach them to come to the fist, but rather to a perch or the ground, only using the fist when manning the bird.

They are intelligent birds and tend to be lazy and so consequently are very difficult to get really fit. They take a very long time to get tame and really relaxed, and can be subject to fits of temper. They should only be flown in eagle country, and if you don't know what that is then don't get an eagle.

GOLDEN EAGLE (*Aquila chrysaetos*)
This is the largest eagle likely to be flown in this country, although there are really very few people in a position to do so. The males are of more use in falconry as they are smaller and more manageable than the females. They will easily take hares, I suppose they will take foxes although I would not want to hunt these with eagles, particularly as eagles are so expensive and hard to get. The thought of a fox biting an eagle and perhaps injuring it badly puts me off completely. As for hunting deer, I don't believe that any eagle can kill deer or antelope cleanly and anything that one hunts should be killed as cleanly and quickly as possible or one should not be hunting it.

Ronnie Moore, who is well known for his female Golden Eagle (and his hat), flies her at rabbits and hares, well away from anyone, very high up in the Yorkshire Dales and he only flies her when the winds are westerly. To have carried Ailsa miles up into the hills, hunted with her, caught, as he did when I was with him, five rabbits and then carried the eagle and over 20lb (9kg) of rabbits down off the hill again, he is, as you can imagine, very fit. I was exhausted. This does give you an idea of how much hard work it is to fly an eagle well.

TAWNY EAGLE (*Aquila rapax*)
Tawny Eagles come from both India and Africa. Here at The NBoP Centre we breed them and I am sure that my pair came originally from India. The African species are larger and 'tend' to be redder in colour, please note that I only say 'tend' to be as there is great colour variation in Tawny Eagles.

I failed to get my pair to rear any of the young until 1991 and as they lay very early I cannot get the young reared by foster parents, so most of our Tawny Eagles have had to be hand reared. This, as with all imprinted birds, makes them more aggressive and less pleasant to handle, but if you are careful with the training they can be quite nice birds. Tawny Eagles are considerably smaller than

Sable, an adult female Golden Eagle

Flash, a Tawny Eagle

Golden Eagles and their supposed subspecies the Steppe Eagle. They are about the only eagle that can be flown in country other than moorland, and will take rabbits easily if the slip is long enough. I have never had time to try them at hares but think that with time and fitness they would be very good. I like Tawnys, and if you have to fly an eagle, this is the one I would recommend, as they are far more versatile than the big eagles.

STEPPE EAGLE (*Aquila rapax nipalensis*)

They have been captive bred in this country by a falconer called R. Crease, which is great. I hope he can keep them breeding regularly.

Why these have been labelled a subspecies of the Tawny Eagle I really can't understand. They are twice the size of the Indian Tawny Eagle and a good deal larger than the African Tawny Eagle and are different in many ways. I don't think they would be as useful a hunting bird as Tawny Eagles as they are almost as large as a Golden Eagle—my female Steppe Eagle flew at only $1/2$lb (225g) less heavy than Ronnie Moore's Golden Eagle—but their feet are comparatively small. They tend to be clumsy birds so you don't gain the manoeuvrability of the smaller Tawny Eagle.

Sarah, our Steppe Eagle, was one of the laziest birds I have ever met, and walked to wherever she wanted to go if given the chance.

BONELLI'S EAGLE (*Hieraatus fasciatus*)
AFRICAN HAWK EAGLE (*Hieraatus fasciatus spilogaster*)

There are a couple of people trying to breed these in captivity over here. They are, of all the eagles, the most useful for falconry. They are truly neither eagles nor hawk eagles but fall between the two. They will fly in almost any countryside, other than really thick woodland, and are brave to the point of being absolutely round the bend. As with the hawk eagles, they take a long time to get flying but don't spend quite so much time deciding to actually move, as the true hawk eagles do. Once they switch on they will chase almost anything and are ideal for hares. They will also take game easily if fit enough.

I have seen them hit rabbits going flat out down steep hills and not even consider about brakes, somersaulting the rest of the way and yet never letting go of the quarry.

As with all eagles, they are temperamental to begin with, but tame well, and are first-class birds in my opinion.

Owls

There is an increasing number of people turning to the eagle owls now as falconry birds. It is not my idea of falconry, but that is not to say that they can't catch quarry.

(*above*) Hodgeson's Hawk Eagle. These birds are no longer available for falconry in this country

(*left*) Sarah, an adult female Steppe Eagle

Adult owls are very, very difficult to train and have to be cut down so hard that I would strongly advise against even attempting one. Most people use birds that have been hand reared from about four weeks old. If you totally hand rear one on its own, from day one, it will be useless for breeding in the future, which is a shame and a waste of a good bird. If, however, you leave them with parents or with siblings for the first three weeks they will still tame down, but will breed at a later date.

I don't like to see owls tethered, and all our flying owls are kept flying free in pens. They work much better if they are loose in a pen. They keep tame by being handled daily while in there.

I have seen some pretty worrying sights at some of the shows I have been to in the last years. There are now a number of people taking injured birds to shows and collecting money in order to help other such birds. I suppose that this is a very laudable reason, but it is not legal and I definitely don't think it is fair on the injured birds, particularly the owls who are not happy in those sort of circumstances. It also causes a fair amount of less than polite comment from some of the public. The most worrying aspect I have seen is the number of tame Barn Owls that have been flown free, still with their leashes on, in places that I would not dream of asking any bird to fly.

Most owls, even the tamest, can be temperamental and don't take kindly to anything out of the normal happening. If the only way you can get your owl to fly is to keep it very hungry all the time, it should not be flown. Birds must be enjoying themselves and like their job, or they should not be asked to do it. We have a few birds here, including some owls, whom we have tried to fly, and they have not been able to fit in with our regime. They very obviously have not been happy so we have stopped flying them. Instead we have put them into pens, for breeding, where they are now having a happy and contented existence. So although owls can be trained and flown, don't fly them if you find that they are not enjoying it.

There are, however, a few people who have done very well indeed with the large eagle owls and caught a respectable number of quarry. I take my hat off to them for perseverance.

EUROPEAN EAGLE OWL (*Bubo bubo*)
This is the largest of all the owls and although I normally don't like to give weights, the males are around $5^1/_2$lb (2.5kg), and the females can go to $7^1/_2$lb (3.5kg) or heavier. They are capable of holding anything up to the size of a hare, particularly the females. They are very powerful and you will need a good eagle glove. They don't seem to be as rapacious as the Great Horned Owls who are their American cousins.

Prairie/Gyr Falcon cross (*Eric & David Hosking*)

There are several different subspecies or races: Indian Eagle Owl (*Bubo bubo bengalensis*), Iranian Eagle Owl (*B.b.nikolskii*), and sometimes Savigny's Eagle Owl (*B.b.ascalaphus*) is also put into this group although I would strongly disagree. All but Savigny's are medium to large, and fairly powerful eagle owls, and all should be able to take rabbits. Savigny's is too small and light to hunt rabbits, and would more than likely be hurt if kicked off by one.

GREAT HORNED OWL (*Bubo virginianus*)
This is a much more aggressive owl, especially when breeding in captivity! I am told that there is a story of a Great Horned Owl killing a human. The story is American: 'A man was going for a walk in the woods late at night. He was wearing a Davy Crockett hat (fur with a tail). As he was walking along, down flew a Great Horned Owl. The owl grabbed the hat, thinking its luck was in and it had finally found the only six-foot high racoon in the United States, and lo and behold, it had managed to kill the man underneath the hat as well.'

Now I have great experience in this field. I once went into our Great Horned Owl's pen to take the first clutch of eggs. I did have a crash helmet, but with my normal forethought, and great stupidity, I put the eggs into the crash helmet—well it seemed like a good idea at the time—and they were kept very safe, believe me; the female Great Horned Owl then belted me over the head, leaving eight holes from eight talons. As can be seen, I lived to tell the tale and I don't think my skull is any thicker than anyone else's. But it sure as hell bleeds well.

I do know of one or two Americans who have flown these birds, and a few people over here. Of all the eagle owls they should be the most useful because of their natural aggression. They are also not quite so heavy to carry around as the European Eagle Owl.

Although there are a few other species of eagle owl being bred in this country, most of them are not suitable for hunting with.

———————

(*above left*) Sam, a Golden Eagle. This photograph was taken in Scotland during filming for Anglia TV's *Survival* programme, hence the lack of jesses on the bird and the rather bare legs
(*below left*) Three-day-old Harris Hawk. This bird was returned to its parents at ten days old

Great Horned Owl—Columbus

European Eagle Owl—Mozart

Snowy Owl

The British Owls
SNOWY OWL (*Nyctea scandiaca*)

This is the only large British owl, and in my experience they are very aggressive birds to handle, even when hand reared. For some reason, I am not sure why, it is my least favourite bird of prey. As they come from above the tree line, they cannot land easily in trees. Because of this they are also very clumsy on the fist and appear to feel uncomfortable. Like the Ferruginous Buzzard, they like open space and room to land where they like. I do not consider them birds that should be jessed and handled.

LITTLE OWL (*Athene noctua*)
This little bird is too bad tempered, once full grown, and too small to train safely. The adults will often die rather than be trained. Hand-reared young will be tame to start with, but generally get wild and unhappy if not handled a great deal every day. They are not, and never will be, falconry birds.

SHORT-EARED OWL and LONG-EARED OWL (*Asio flammeus* and *Asio otus*)
These would be of no use in falconry and, as I know of no one breeding them, they are not available.

TAWNY OWL and BARN OWL (*Strix aluco* and *Tyto alba*))
Again these are relatively small birds and of little use to the falconer. Tawny Owls are only bred in captivity infrequently; they

Owls can look miserable when tethered. They are best kept loose in a pen

Tawny Owl

seem to be quite difficult to breed. Barn Owls on the other hand are very easy to breed. This is not always good for the Barn Owl. They are cheap to buy and, sadly, a lot of them are ending up as pets or beginner's birds to unsuitable people. I thoroughly agree with Emma Ford, who has written three books on falconry, when she says that 'owls make totally unsuitable pets being both messy and a great tie'. I would add to that statement in that I don't believe they are particularly happy as pets.

So, if you must hunt with an owl, use one of the eagle owls and leave the rest. Or have them just for captive breeding, or as friends in a nice pen. But apart from a total imprint owl, they are generally sociable birds, and it is not kind to keep them alone.

Two words of warning with owls. Firstly they can be *very* noisy. All the eagle owls will hoot and call throughout the night, especially during the breeding season, even if they are kept alone. The noise will carry for at least a mile on a still night. Tawny Owls are even

Kestrel

worse in the noise stakes. Not only do they screech like a banshee, sounding like rape and murder at 3am, but they will attract wild ones as well. We have had up to twelve owls calling to one another and bouncing up and down on top of the aviary wire. All this noise is not conducive to good neighbourhood relationships. I have known of several cases where owners have had to get rid of their owls because of complaints to the police or the council about disturbances. One can hardly blame the neighbours. If you live in close proximity to others, don't try keeping owls. Or if you absolutely must keep owls, move house.

The second thing to be wary about is that hand-reared owls can get possessive with their owners and very dangerous to spouses or children. A friend of mine has a female eagle owl (he did swear blind that it was male until it laid eggs). This bird caused his wife to be taken to hospital when it attacked her as she walked past where the bird was tethered. It would almost certainly do the same thing if they had children. Never keep a mature tame eagle owl tethered. Keep it in a safe pen where children and strangers cannot get within reach.

Kestrel (*Falco tinnunculus*)

You may wonder why I haven't discussed this bird until now. Well, most of us don't consider it a bird suitable for falconry. It is a lovely bird, marvellous to watch fly in the wild and a very sweet bird in captivity. They make very good aviary birds. But, they are small, and they make lousy beginner's birds. Once past the beginner stage, there are very few people who want to fly them. They are not persistent at the lure as they do not hunt like other falcons, so for flying to the lure for fun they are not good. They hunt mice, beetles and the like so as a hunting bird they are pretty much not on, though we have on occasion caught things with Kestrels here. Our best bag was seventeen worms in one afternoon with only one bird. I know there are a very few people who have caught quarry with them, and have even heard of one bird catching a pheasant, but these are the exceptions rather than the rule and so they are not generally used as a falconry bird.

Hobby (*Falco subbuteo*)

A couple of people have now bred Hobbies. We are trying to breed them and have had eggs, but no fertile ones as yet. They are not a falconry bird as they only hunt other birds when they have young to feed, otherwise they are insectivorous.

3 MAKING A START

Assuming that you are going to take up falconry or wish to rethink the way you house your birds, you will need numerous items to look after any bird well. These will allow you freedom from worry should you be away during the day; solve the problem of all extremes of weather affecting your bird; and enable you to cope with the bird should it, at any time, become sick or injured. Following is what I consider vital to keep a bird well and safe, allowing for most things that can happen:

a safe pen which doubles as a sheltered weathering ground to have the bird tethered, and an aviary to have it loose. This does not necessarily have the same requirements as a pen designed for captive breeding (see Chapter 5).

a reasonable sized shed or building, so that you have somewhere safe, secure and warm in case of extreme cold, for a bird that is down in weight, sick or injured.

The Pen/Weathering Ground

Unless you are flying large numbers of birds as we are here at the Centre, it is better by far to keep your bird loose in a pen, once it is trained and tame. When I first got married, and I was away from the Centre for eighteen months, I kept my birds loose

in pens (while still flying them daily) even through the bad winter
in 1981 and the birds did very well, probably far better than they
would have done had they been tethered. You may find that if
you build a really nice pen, the bird will show signs of breeding
even while you are flying it. I cannot recommend too highly that
it is always best to keep most flying birds loose in a safe pen if
possible, rather than tethered.

As with aviaries (see Chapter 4) build for the worst of everything
happening—all weather conditions, children throwing stones at the
birds, etc. A friend of ours had his beautiful Imperial Eagle stoned
to death in his garden in this country. Build so the bird is safe from
foxes, cats, dogs, badgers, mink, magpies, crows and humans. Most
of these can kill a bird up to the size of a female Goshawk; magpies
and crows can steal food and your bird may only be getting a third
of the food that you are giving it. Rats are capable of killing small
hawks and falcons. In the United States, Great Horned Owls have
been known on numerous occasions to kill tethered birds. In this
country it is unlikely that this would happen as our owls are much
smaller. However a Tawny Owl is capable of killing Sparrowhawks,
Kestrels and Merlins if they are left unprotected at night.

Humans may well release a bird, either because they mistakenly
think it wrong to tether birds, or just for the hell of it. Theft of
birds is important to protect against, as is the injuring of birds
by vandals, which has been known. Another friend of ours came
home one evening to find his house burgled and his two American
Kestrels, which were tethered on the lawn, badly hurt. The thieves
had broken the birds' wings and legs and left them there, still living.
I am only glad I never knew who did it or I would have done exactly
the same thing to them.

SIZE
Size is vital, if having a bird tethered. The minimum for the smallest
bird is 6ft (1.9m) wide by 12ft (3.6m) deep. I would suggest that the
lowest height built is above human height, thus avoiding cracked
skulls. For preference I would build weathering grounds at least 8ft
(2.4m) high. If housing large falcons, buzzards or hawks, the width
should be at least 10ft (3m) to stop wings touching the sides, 16ft
(4.9m) deep and 8ft (2.4m) high. Eagles should be given at least
15ft (4.5m) in width and 20ft (6m) from back to front, preferably
10ft (3m) in height.

FOUNDATIONS
Starting with the ground-work, build good foundations. Whatever
the structure to be built, it will last longer if placed on a concrete-block
foundation wall. Put a damp proof course on top of the blocks before

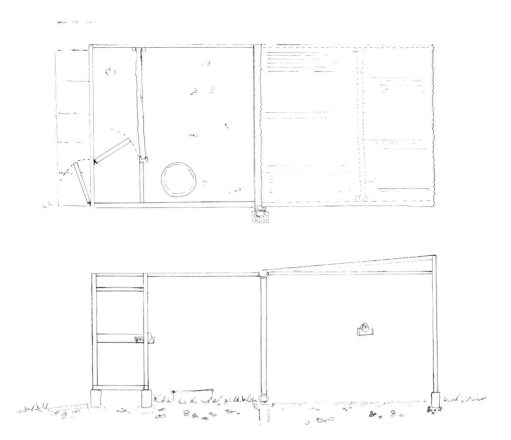

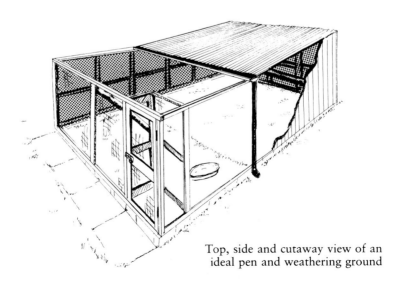

Top, side and cutaway view of an
ideal pen and weathering ground

building on up. The wall, as in our breeding pens, will stop the risk of rats, dogs or foxes digging underneath into your weathering ground, injuring or killing the bird, or making escape holes available.

SIDES
The sides of the quarters should be solid, all but the front. Facing south is best, but more important than that is that the birds should be able to see plenty going on from their quarters, reducing boredom and keeping the bird tamer. If the weather gets bad during the winter a plastic sheet can be battened onto the front. This will stop freezing winds and driving snow affecting the bird.

The sides can be built of all sorts of materials. Block-work can be continued up from the foundations; brick could be used, looking superb but very costly. Timber is probably the best choice for most people. However I would strongly advise against fence panels. Put up a decent framework and cover it with $1/2$in (1.25cm) x 6in (15cm) feather edge treated that will last you years, and be far more secure.

FRONT
The front should be covered with a thick gauge weldmesh or twilweld wire. I don't know if there is a plastic-coated weldmesh type wire of thick gauge. If there was, this would be ideal. If the wire is painted black with a bitumen paint it is much easier to see through and view the bird. Plastic-coated chain link is also a good material.

DOORS
Incorporate a double-door system. It is not safe to have just a single door. The bird, if loose, could nip past you, however tame. Make it wide and high enough for comfortable entry and preferably wide enough to push a wheelbarrow through for cleaning.

FLOOR COVERING
The reason I suggest a deep weathering ground is that I like to have it half sheltered and half open and grassed. It is vital to have a safe grass area on which to place young, newly jessed birds. They cannot hurt themselves while fighting the new jesses if they are on grass. Sand, peat or gravel can injure a bird that is struggling against the jesses for the first couple of days. We leave all our young birds on the grassed area for about a week until they have settled, only putting them on the sand area if the weather turns bad at night.

The other half of the pen is covered in about 6in (15cm) of silver sand, if you can get it, or dune sand. You can use builder's sand which is cheaper, but it may turn the bird a lovely pink, or possibly yellow depending on the colour of the sand. I have seen gravel used, but I don't like it for tethered birds as I think it is a little hard. If gravel is to be used, only use pea gravel which is rounded—and expensive. Peat dries out quickly, and becomes very dusty.

It is better always to place the bath on the grassed area, keeping the sand dry and the bird much cleaner.

ROOFING
At least half the pen should be roofed. It should be well shaded and not let through too much light. Overheating kills birds far quicker than cold and a tethered bird cannot move out of the sun. For choice I would use Onduline. Put a good gutter to take away excess water. The other half can be roofed either in nylon netting (see Chapter 4) or weldmesh/twilweld, again using a thick gauge.

PERCHES
If the bird is to be tethered, the perch will go centrally on the sand and similarly on the grass. If you are going to let it loose once it is tame, trained and settled, other perches will have to be placed in the pen. As you will need to tether the bird again at some time, the perches should be easily removable. They cannot be left in when the bird is re-tethered or it will constantly bate at them. One long perch under the shelter, centrally placed in wooden cups, and another towards the front should be fine.

NUMBER OF BIRDS
It is inadvisable to have more than one bird tethered in a pen. It only needs one of them to get loose and the result may well be $1^1/_2$ birds instead of 2. If you are housing more than one bird, double the width of the quarters and put a solid dividing wall between the birds.

One of the few times we have had a complaint about one of our birds screaming was from a gentleman who had cut down his young bird (it was still not yet feeding on the fist, but getting close). He then threw food to a Kestrel right next door, and in full view of his hungry young bird. Hardly surprising that his young bird was upset and screamed at the Kestrel for food. If one bird is cut down in weight, it is unkind and unwise to feed another in front of it.

PATHS
To avoid the weathering area getting dirty, make a good gravel, concrete or paving-stone path to it. Then, the constant use will not mean that you are ploughing through mud during wet weather to get to your bird. It will also be easier to clear snow from during prolonged bad spells.

SECURITY
Don't forget a good lock on the outside door. I would suggest a Yale?type lock, they are less likely to freeze up than the conventional padlock. If you can afford it some sort of security system is a good idea, particularly with the increase in bird prices and the increase in the animal liberation movement. Loose birds need not be put in during cold weather, but tethered birds, particularly Lanners, Luggers and Harries Hawks, should not be left out.

HYGIENE
ALWAYS keep weathering grounds clean. Rake out and remove soiled sand daily. Have a compost heap with all soiled materials well away from where the bird is kept. Loose birds need not be put in during cold weather, but tethered birds, particularly Lanners, Luggers and Harris Hawks should not be left out.

The Shed

The shed or building for housing a bird indoors should be at least 10ft×10ft (3m×3m), giving you room to put in a sick/night quarter, plus all the equipment you will need for the bird itself. The following is what I would consider to be essential:

- A fridge for keeping food fresh and a small deep freeze to keep enough supplies of food so that you will never run out in emergencies.
- A night/sick quarter should your bird ever need to be put in because of injury, illness or very bad weather. Don't use a tea chest, build a proper box for the job, that is easy to clean, and can't hurt the bird in any way. Put vertical bars on the door. Information can be found in *Falconry and Hawking* by P. Glasier.
- A good weighing machine and weights. It is vital to check these regularly. I have known scales go out of true and kill birds because they were not checked. Never rely just on your weighing machine. Use it in conjunction with feeling and handling the bird to know how fat, or thin, or fit, it is.
- A sturdy small table on which to put the weighing machine, and to work on.
- A medicine cupboard for emergency supplies.
- Another cupboard for keeping leather, tools and various odds and sods.
- Hooks for hanging hoods, gloves, bags and unwanted intruders etc.
- A blackboard or wall chart for keeping weighing and performance records.
- Storage space for travelling perches, a travelling box for emergencies and so on.
- Running water and a sink.
- Electricity for lighting and heating. (Only use electricity for heating, gas or paraffin can have dangerous fumes which may affect birds.)

You may well need a bigger shed!

Simon (and Asterix) recording daily weights on the blackboard

A good weighing machine is vital

Equipment for the Bird Itself

JESSES

I don't like false Aylmeri as I have had birds catch their talons in the eyelet. Be careful to get the correct sized, well-prepared true Aylmeri as, if the eyelet is too big for the size of bird, it will wear on the back of the bird's leg and produce a very nasty sore. Watch out for Aylmeri on tiny falcons such as Kestrels and Merlins; they are very good at pulling the leather out of the eyelet. Aylmeri are better for birds than traditional jesses as they can't get hooked up in anything while the bird is hunting, as hunting straps are used. But Aylmeri are more inclined to break simultaneously and can, as stated, injure the bird if they are the wrong size or fitted badly. I still use traditional jesses, with short straps on some of my birds, particularly the falcons and true Aylmeri on the rest of the birds.

Tip: grease the jesses daily using Ko-cho-line. It is available from any saddlery shop, and it does not rot the leather too much. Throw the jesses away after a season's use. Why risk them breaking just for the price of a new pair?

SWIVELS

Some are good, others are bad. Sometimes you can just be unlucky and they break for no good reason. As with jesses and leashes, this problem points to the wisdom of having the bird in a pen, whether tethered or not. In this way, even if the equipment fails, the bird cannot go anywhere. I don't like the American barrel swivels except for the tiny ones that I use on my lureline; the jesses slip down onto the rings too easily, then the bird gets tangled. We use the D-type swivels obtainable from Martin Jones, also Robin Haigh's Hawkmaster swivels, both of which we find are okay.

Tip: always have several spares.

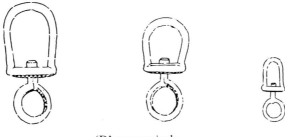

'D' type swivels

LEASHES

Anyone who still uses the old rawhide leather leashes is round the bend and irresponsible in my opinion. You cannot tell when they are wearing out and they can snap without warning. If you lose a bird that is tethered with one of these it serves you right. The irresponsibility is that unless you find the bird, or it is very lucky, it will probably get hung up and may even die. The only bird we had to use a leather leash on was our old Changeable Hawk Eagle, Brimstone, who unravelled anything else. Now we keep her retired in a pen and don't have the problem. Braided terylene is the material to use.

Tip: check the knot very regularly and keep leashes clean.

BELLS

The best bells I have seen, or rather heard, are Steve Little bells from the United States. They sound wonderful and are lovely to look at as well. Next come Asborno bells, also American but difficult to get. Barry Osthuizen makes good bells in Zimbabwe but he finds the materials difficult to obtain. Last but not least come the Indian bells, which are not always good and so have to be checked for sound. As they are made of far thinner material they do not last well.

Tip: we tail-bell all the birds we can, including the falcons. The bells last far longer, don't get in the way on falcon's stubby legs, and ring better, they can be heard from a greater distance.

HOODS

Although I do occasionally make my own hoods, lack of time means that we usually buy them. There are four main types. The Arab style, funnily enough, fits our Sakers better than others and the birds seem more comfortable in them as well. I like the less gaudy ones, but that is just a matter of taste. The Dutch style is difficult to make needing a block as does The Falconry Centre style. I prefer our own model to the Dutch, it seems to fit better and more comfortably over the eyes. Both styles will last better than any other; both have lasted years here and they get treated very hard. The Anglo-Indian are the easiest to make and are fine to use, but they tend not to fit as well as the other three.

The Americans make superb hoods, sewing them together with dental floss. Dug Pineo makes, probably, the best of all. I would very much like to learn their techniques one day, when I have the time. However, the hoods over here are good, comfortable for the birds and they work, which is the main thing.

Probably the most important tip I can offer, with hoods, is that they do not make a bird tame. I don't like to see birds left hooded for hours. I don't think it is kind and it doesn't get you or the bird anywhere. Although it is useful to make most birds used to the hood

Jo with a young falcon on the creance. We get birds off the line as quickly as possible

A falcon with a Dutch hood

so that you can use one if you need to, do not over use them. The more sights you let your bird see, the better bird it will become. It will be happier, more confident and less easy to lose. Make sure that whatever you use, it fits the bird well.

You can't hood owls and it is unnecessary to hood small falcons.

Hoods if used incorrectly can kill birds. Don't hood a bird that has not cast (brought up a pellet from the food eaten the previous day), or one with food in its crop. If the bird is sick and tries to vomit through its hood, it can easily choke to death. Never put a hooded bird down anywhere without securing it. Such birds can, and will, fly off hooded. Their chances if this happens are very slim. It should never be allowed to happen.

CREANCES
Don't use any old piece of string or twine, get the proper material. Why risk the bird for a fiver at most? Braided terylene is good, of varying thickness depending on the bird you are going to train. I like the stick tied securely to the end of the line, preferably with the line going through a hole drilled in the stick. You have no idea how many times I have seen the line run through someone's hands and slip out of their grasp because there was no stop at the end. Be careful, with a powerful bird pulling the line through your hand you can get a very nasty burn from the line.

Dragged Creances I don't like them, I never use them, I won't let my staff use them, I consider them dangerous. In the age of telemetry they are out-dated, and can upset a bird unnecessarily in the early stages of training.

LURES AND LINES
If you are going to swing a lure to any degree of accuracy or expertise, the line should be braided cotton. This will not burn your hand. People use all sorts of different things as a lure. I think some of the Americans are tops for the most amazing. I have see one brochure where the lure is a complete life-size model of whatever bird you want to hunt. How the hell you swing it, I just don't know, and for heaven's sake don't accidentally hit your bird with it, death would be instantaneous. Don't hit yourself with it either—the result

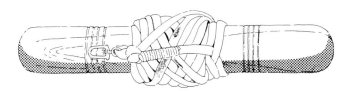

A lure line

could well be the same. I did hear of one chap in this country using a small yellow teddy bear as a lure, presumably because it was the same colour as a day-old chick—poor behaviour in my opinion.

Don't just tie chicks to a line, it looks extremely bad as far as any outsider to falconry is concerned, is unprofessional, and the chick will fall to pieces after a very short time or if the bird touches it. Remember that you are responsible for the public image of falconry wherever you are. It makes no difference if you are flying a bird for the public professionally or just training one privately for yourself, people may well still see what you are doing.

We use a pair of moorhen or magpie wings, dried in an open position, and tied back to back. They swing better than bigger wings. We then tie on a fresh piece of tough beef each day. In this way the bird gets instant reward when it catches the lure, which is light enough not to hurt the bird should you touch it by accident, and lasts well while the bird is feeding as you make in. By remaking the lure each day you also check that the line is not worn, and the meat is securely tied.

Tip: make sure that the stick is heavy enough for the bird not to carry the lure too far, but not too heavy so that it might injure the bird. Paint it a good bright colour (not red) so that you can find it easily in long grass or heather.

Dummy Rabbits Pretty basic affairs really: I have made many of the damn things. Always make them after at least three gin and tonics. The only point you have to be aware of is that if you make the dummy bunny too round it will roll when the bird grabs it, and this can cause broken tail feathers. Always put a nice lot of meat dressing on the rabbit to start with, so that the bird gets plenty of reward in the early stages, thus encouraging it greatly.

FALCONRY BAGS

It does not really matter what you use as long as you remember two things. Firstly, the bag will need two compartments, so that when you pull out the lure, you do not pull out the pick-up piece as well. If this happens, the bird is more than likely to grab the fallen piece of meat and disappear with it, leaving you feeling like a pratt of the first order. Secondly, the bag should be easy to keep clean —for the health of the bird.

GLOVES

Although you can make gloves yourself, good leather is so hard to find that it is much easier to buy them. Martin Jones makes the best I have seen in any country so far. You will only need a short glove for small falcons, small hawks or small owls. A longer single-thickness is necessary for large falcons, a double-thickness

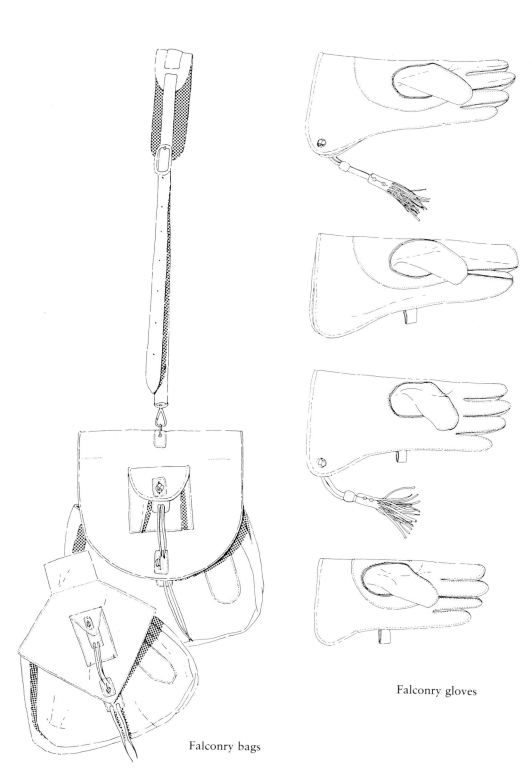

Falconry bags

Falconry gloves

for all buzzards, large hawks and eagle owls and an eagle glove for eagles.

Keep your glove as clean as possible for the health of the bird. You have got to be out of your mind if you feed day-old chicks on the fist regularly. They ruin an expensive glove quicker than almost anything. Keep all gloves away from dogs; they love them.

BLOCKS

There are various types of blocks, most of which are fine. I like uneven cork on the top of ours as it is easy to clean, warm for the birds' feet in cold weather, and fairly soft and bouncy. You can also use Astroturf, but this needs cleaning almost daily as it collects dirt easily, I don't use it and don't like it. I also don't like flat tops on my blocks, they are not as comfortable as rounded uneven topped ones.

You must always check that the top is not so narrow as to let the jesses slip down either side, thus causing the bird to straddle the block. We use blocks with a metal rod showing about 6in (15cm) above the ground, before the wooden stand. The ring moves fairly freely round this rod. The reason I use this kind is that if, by any chance, a falcon does straddle the block, all it will do is possibly damage its tail feathers against the rod. If the block is wide wood all the way to the ground, the bird's body is held up tightly against it. We had a bird die from injured kidneys because of this. Remember though, we are probably a special case when it comes to equipment as we have up to thirty flying birds tethered during the summer, and so whatever we work with has to be designed for use with a lot of

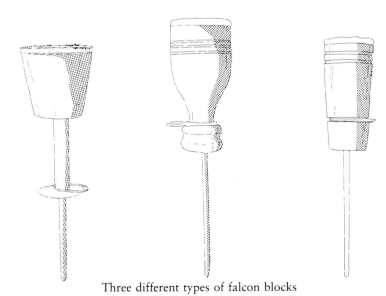

Three different types of falcon blocks

A well-padded indoor or outdoor perch

birds. Still, birds getting tangled up occasionally is a normal part of falconry—yet another good reason to keep your flying bird loose in a pen if you are able.

It doesn't really matter what sort of block you use as long as it is safe, and comfortable for the bird. I still have not found the perfect block. Just make sure that whatever you have in the end, you keep it clean.

PERCHES

Bow Perches We have tried a number of different designs. I don't really like the ones with a branch as the bow, partly because it is not 100 per cent safe and partly because, as the timber seasons, it gets very hard for the bird's feet. I prefer a metal bow, made as part of the whole structure with a nicely padded, leather gripping-area for the bird—especially for birds such as Sparrowhawks, who have softer and more delicate skin than other birds. The best padding is extruded foam pipe-lagging that you can buy in metre lengths. It is soft and insulates the birds' feet in freezing weather. The problem with a padded area is that, if it is not done well, the ring can get caught on it. Still, this is the type I prefer to use.

Ring Perches I don't like them and I never use them.
Perches for Eagles We use very large bow perches, many of which

we have had for years. We also like to have a large rock or log as an alternative perch. You can use something similar to one of those ground, screw-in dog ties, but much better made. This will hold into the ground without moving and the bird can be tethered to it easily. Don't forget it's there when you mow the grass, however, as it will write off a lawnmower very quickly.

I am not really happy with the various perches we have, and would like to alter all our perching for the trained birds in the Hawk Walk. We are going to rebuild the whole thing, one day when funds allow. However I am not 100 per cent sure of what I want to do yet in the way of different perching, or if my ideas will work. Several of my American friends keep their birds on a rather good indoor system, which I think might work outside, under a shelter. They have a half circle of wood, covered in carpet on the base, as a shelf on a wall. The bird can fly onto it and the area is large enough, not only for the bird to sit comfortably but to lie down if it wishes. I like this idea as many of my birds like to lie down. The bird cannot get tangled and is tethered to a fixing below where the wall meets either the floor or, when indoors, a wide table-like shelf.

I would like to do the same sort of thing on the back wall of each compartment putting the half-circle shelf about 2ft (60cm) off the ground, giving the bird a little height, which most birds like. The bird would be tethered to a fixing at the bottom of the wall, or maybe in the centre of the compartment. I would then like each bird to have the choice of two perching positions by giving a second perch in the form of a large rock or log, carefully positioned, towards the front of the compartment. We would have to make sure that the bird did not damage its feathers by hitting the forward perch. Birds in the early stages of training would have to have the more traditional perches, until they were steady enough to be moved to the new system. I don't know if it will work, but I think it will.

BATHS

The baths I liked best were the galvanised pigeon baths produced by Eltex in Worcester and these are sadly no longer made. There are numerous people making baths from glass fibre. These are fine, if the edge is not too sharp. If the edges can be made nice and wide it is much more comfortable for the bird's feet and better for it as well. Birds should be offered baths at least four times a week, every day if the weather is hot. Birds in a free condition in a pen should always have a bath available. Many birds will not bath, but should still be given the option if they are tethered. We have a Kestrel here who, immediately he is offered a bath, opens his wings to dry himself—he has never been known to get in. Nevertheless he is always offered one.

Thumbs, a Lanner, with his bath

Do not let birds bath during the afternoon in freezing conditions. I have heard of several birds that have frozen to death in the cold winters we have been having recently because idiots let them bath in the afternoon, thus not giving them time to dry before the sun went down. As birds will generally bath when the bath has just been refilled, make sure that you refill it early morning during the winter and, if possible, remove it at lunchtime. With aviary birds, the bath may not be removable; but if it is never refilled unless the sun is out, and then only in the morning, they will not normally bath. The bath will be frozen if the weather is really cold. Don't worry about this.

If the birds were in the wild in that weather the water would also be frozen and they would be unlikely to get a bath until the weather had improved. The birds most likely to bath during the winter are Peregrines and Sparrowhawks, although many of the birds that live in climates similar to ours may also do so.

If by any chance a tethered bird does get wet during the afternoon, or is not dry before nightfall, bring it in for the night and dry it with a hair dryer. Be careful not to overheat the bird, and leave it indoors in its night quarters until next morning. It would be unwise to warm a bird up with a hair dryer and then put it outside in the cold immediately.

Food

It never fails to amaze me that people will go out and buy a bird without sorting out a food supply first. I believe it is bad practice to feed birds on any one diet. We use a mixture of good beef for training and feeding on the fist, day-old cockerels, quail, rats, mice and rabbits.

DOCs have plenty of egg yolk which will provide plenty of moisture for the bird. It is interesting to note how often all birds will first eat/drink the yolk before eating the rest. As feeding DOCs on the fist is messy, we feed on the ground. There is a school of thought that says you should only feed a bird on the fist. We do not subscribe to this, for if you are not careful, it is possible to have birds such as Merlins refusing to feed unless you pick them up. This is not good policy. DOCs are not a good enough diet on their own, particularly for the *accipiters*, especially when they are being flown. All the hawks, even the tamest, use a tremendous amount of nervous energy, and they need a good high protein diet.

Quail suit the hawks well, with DOCs once or twice a week for the moisture content. If given to small birds such as Merlins, who are much more inclined to breed on a good quality diet, quail should be gutted and cut in half, perhaps even quarters, so they can carry it. In fact most of my falcons leave the guts. If you find that a bird never eats them you might as well gut first to save clearing up later. There is no need to feed the buzzard family vast amounts of expensive quail, as they will be just as happy on a lower-protein food source, but they and eagles benefit from the occasional rabbit. This is good for their beaks, feet and muscles.

Falcons tend not to like rats (I'm not over keen on them myself), but eagles, buzzards and the large owls do well on them and they are a more natural diet. Mice are probably the most difficult food to get anything to eat. Many birds, especially if they have been fed DOCs for a long time, will not go over to mice unless they get pretty hungry, so choose a good time of year to introduce them. Late summer, early autumn is best.

Always make sure that birds, particularly small birds in pens, will eat more that one diet. If, by any chance, your food source lets you down and you have to change diets during bad weather, birds may take too long to get used to the new food and get into dangerously low condition, they may even die. To avoid this all birds should be got used to a varied diet.

Never refreeze food, any more than you should do with food for your own consumption. Don't feed food that has been picked up off the side of the road (road casualties). How can you know that it wasn't run over because it was ill or poisoned? Don't feed food that has been shot with a shotgun—lead kills. Rabbits killed with a .22 rifle are okay if the bullet has passed straight through and out.

Falconers and zoos have been very lucky for years with the price of food for their birds. Sadly this has led to some people refusing to pay more for the better quality and relatively expensive food such as quail. Even feeding quail every day (which I have suggested is not a good idea) it will still only cost about £3.50 a week for a bird up to the size of a Goshawk or Redtail. Work out how much your dog costs and you will see that the prices are not far off. If good quality birds are to be achieved, good quality feeding should be done. Doing things on the cheap is never a good idea.

Veterinary Care

Apart from sorting out good food supplies, the other vital aspect to get fixed up before a bird arrives, is a good vet. I have been told by several people that they have been turned away by vets. This may be a good thing, because if that particular vet is not interested, he or she will probably not be the man (or woman) for the job anyway. Firstly find out if you have a vet close by who is known for expertise in treating raptors, if not, the local vet should be approached. Ask him if he will take on the care of the bird in question. If the vet is not experienced (ask him) then it is very important that he will confer with a vet known for experience. If I had to move now, and didn't have one of the super vets we have round us here, I would ask my new vet if he (or she) would mind phoning up the vet I named, to ask for advice on whatever the problem was. If he was not prepared to do this I would find one that was.

New Birds

There will come a time with every falconer or breeder when he or she will get a new bird. Whether this bird has been captive bred in this country or imported from abroad the same rules should apply. These are a few tips to go on with before even getting to the stage of collecting a bird:

1 Do your homework on the breeder you are intending to use. Make sure that there is no history of inherited problems with any of his or her birds.
2 I would *strongly* advise against buying a bird from a dealer, ie someone who has bought large numbers of birds in bulk from breeders and is selling them on for a higher price. You will never know what you are getting and your recourse to the law, should things go wrong, will be very much more difficult. Go direct to breeders and let us get rid of dealers altogether.
3 Get a guarantee if you are in the slightest bit worried about a bird. If the breeder will not give you a reasonable guarantee, don't buy the bird.
4 If you are worried about health, get the bird vetted before you buy it.
5 Make sure of the price.
6 Make sure that the paperwork is available, or if for some reason it is not, get a signed piece of paper stating why not.
7 Take a good look at the bird before it goes into the box.

COLLECTING A BIRD
You would not believe what people bring to put birds in when collecting them—baskets that could be seen through by a blind bat, cardboard boxes that would be pushed to hold anything as large as a kitten, and so dilapidated that one flap of a bird's wings and they would disintegrate. Sometimes people bring nothing at all, and very few put a piece of carpet on the floor of the box so the bird will not slip. And all this to put in a bird that might have cost them up to £2000 or perhaps more—amazing!

Take a good large box, bigger than you think the bird will need. I have already suggested that a good wooden box should always be ready in case you need it for travelling a sick bird, and perhaps this is the time to build it. After all, if you can't afford to build a good box, you certainly won't be able to afford a good bird. However if a cardboard box has to be used, electrical shops usually have really good ones that their equipment comes in, and they are large and very strong. If they are not keen offer them £1 for the box. Don't then weaken the box by putting huge holes in it for air. Very few boxes are airtight anyway; a small line of holes around the top will be fine. Line the floor of the box with old clean carpet; not shagpile—that can catch in the bird's talons. I don't like sacking—it slips and can snag a bird's feet. Cut the carpet to fit the box well and the bird will travel well.

Do not expect the breeder to put jesses on for you. Leather is hard to get hold of and I certainly don't give any of mine away. Most probably don't have the time to do it anyway. The bird will have to be handled to get it out of the box so it is just as easy to jess it up then with a friend to help you, when you get home. As we suggest not handling the bird immediately, this may not arise anyway.

Once you start your journey home don't stop for hours at pubs or cafes. Get on with the journey and *never never* leave the box in the sun while in the car. I know of one bird that was dead in the box within ten miles of the start of the journey, due to overheating. Overheating will kill birds far quicker than cold. Try to make sure that you are going to arrive home during daylight hours. It gives the bird a little time to settle before dark. If you arrive after full dark, I would leave the bird in the box somewhere safe and cool until the next morning.

Any new arrival should be released into a pen. A mute sample should be collected immediately, a second one a week later. For the mute sample, plastic can be placed under a used perch in the pen and collected the next morning. These samples should then be placed in a sterile container and taken to the local poultry laboratories for testing both for worms and bacteria. This will give a good indication of the bird's health. If you look in the Yellow Pages phone book under Poultry Laboratories which are often government testing stations, you will find the nearest one to you.

As the bird may have come from a solid-walled breeding pen, it is a good idea to put a sheet of builder's plastic with battens on the inside of the front of the pen, before releasing the bird into it. The bird will not crash then and, if it does in the first day, it will not hurt itself. Once the bird is taken up for training the plastic can be removed, along with the perches. An imported bird will go straight into quarantine quarters, which should be ideal. The mute samples can be collected in the same way.

The bird should be fed up with as much as it will eat for at least two weeks. Never cut down a bird's weight as soon as it arrives. Give it time to settle, get over the stress of a new home and relax. With a new bird, particularly an imported one, unless you know what it has been fed on previously, you may have to try different food types before discovering what it is happy with. Until it is settled with you, it is probably best not to change its diet.

As any bird that has been imported will be looked at by a vet on its arrival at the quarantine station, any noticeable problems should be spotted immediately. This is no bad practice and the same can be done with a new bird from this country. If there is any cause for worry, a blood sample should be taken, by a vet, and he will send it away for analysis. Because there are, sadly, some breeders who are not doing things in the most desirable way, inbreeding is probably causing some of the problems that we are seeing in both Harris Hawks and Ferruginous Buzzards. There are at least three lines of Harris Hawk that I know of which appear to have congenital problems.

Some breeders may not tell the truth as to a bird's method of rearing. This I know through experience. Hand rearing is without doubt safer than allowing parents to do the bulk of rearing. Once the birds are back with the parents, accidents can happen. Because of this occasional loss, some breeders prefer to totally hand rear or crèche rear. I am not totally against some crèche-reared birds. Owls seem to do all right with this method. But it is not the ideal by any means and I personally would not buy a crèche-reared falcon, hawk or buzzard. Although you can breed from crèche-reared birds, if you are lucky, many are very likely to show the unpleasant side of imprinting if being flown.

If the prospective buyer is shown young grouped in a pen they will probably appear wild and thus perhaps parent reared; but only when the bird's weight is cut down can signs of poor rearing techniques really be seen. To safeguard yourself, find out what you can of breeders' reputations.

It never really pays to cut corners and produce poor-quality birds. Most experienced falconers know exactly which breeders they would not buy birds from. Eventually, one hopes, those producing poor birds get known, and start to have problems in disposing of their young stock. Watch out for cheaper-than-market-price birds. It can be a guide. If one goes out to buy a Labrador, most sensible people will check that the line does not have any known hip problems. If buying a horse most people have the animal vetted before even paying for it. Perhaps in this day and age we should do the same if we are not happy about a bird. The vetting will of course have to be payed for by the prospective buyer, and permission and appointments made with the breeder.

Ask for a written guarantee that the bird is not imprinted. If you find that a breeder is not prepared to do this, don't buy the bird. To be of any use, the guarantee should last eight weeks, giving time for imprinting to show. Perhaps at this stage I had better explain a little of what we have learnt about imprinting and imprints.

IMPRINTING
I can't think of any good reason for purposefully imprinting a bird other than to use it for artificial breeding. Therefore most of what I will discuss will be with that in mind.

Imprinting is a totally natural process. Generally speaking, it is the way that wild birds and animals keep the species pure. The young creature imprints on its parents during the first few weeks of its life, then, later, when it has become independent, and is ready to breed itself, it responds to other creatures just like its parents, who make the same vocal responses and are visually the same. In this way blackbirds don't go off and pal up with the nearest thrush, or kestrels with merlins, thus avoiding havoc. If a young bird of prey is reared by a human the bird goes through exactly the same processes, except that it thinks it is a human. To add to that, it never goes through the growing-up period of leaving the parents and gaining independence. It will remain to all intents and purposes a baby all its life, although it may reach breeding condition.

Imprinting covers various different behaviour patterns in birds of prey. All will eventually be implemented in the breeding process. They vary in the different family groups, although probably more is known on imprinting falcons because more has been done in this field. Young birds will imprint most readily on food, then they will imprint sexually on the provider of that food. To imprint a bird well means that it must imprint on the person destined to be its future mate and must not be imprinted through food but through consistent contact, confidence and affection.

It is all too easy to imprint a bird incorrectly, making it unpleasant, unlikely to want to breed with a human, and possibly dangerous. A badly imprinted bird will scream incessantly for food, and snatch at the supposed parent for it. He or she can become aggressive if food is withheld, exactly as it does in the wild with the true parent. With increasing age the bird becomes more and more unpleasant to deal with.

But, and it is a big but, we don't know all there is to know about imprinting yet. There is a difference between imprint behaviour and eyass behaviour. We had one experience last year which emphasises this and how little we really know. One of the young wild Peregrines at the eyrie near us was shot a few days after her first flight. The bird was found and brought to us. She was put in the sick quarters and treated but not handled, other than to examine her and keep her clean. Once recovered, she was trained to see how she could manage serious flying after a prolonged rest. She was not tamed, or handled, other than the minimum needed to get her flying loose and returning—we kept her with so little handling that she was a pig to pick up. The idea in mind was that as she was later to be sent off and returned to the wild, she must not be allowed to become too tame. The interesting fact was that this bird mantled (hid her food with wings, body and tail) quite badly both on the fist and on the ground. She never screamed or got nasty, but she did mantle over food to quite a degree. There was no way this bird was imprinted. She was hatched and reared in the wild and did not even meet mankind until she was full grown and hard down. Mantling need not be a sign of imprinting if screaming does not accompany it.

Just to really complicate matters, some falcons will begin to talk to you while being handled. Many of my birds, falcons particularly, will chat away while catching their breath between flights. They may even scream hello if they see me during the day. They are definitely not screamers, I would not keep them if they were. They don't scream consistently for hours at a time, or even minutes, but they do like to have a quick chat during the day. Neither the odd noise from a bird, nor mantling, are necessarily signs of imprinting unless they are extreme.

There are some who imprint birds on purpose, usually for later use in artificial breeding. In the United States, it is a legal requirement to imprint all hybrid birds to stop the risk of them breeding with wild populations should they get lost, although there is little proof of this ever happening.

The Americans have perfected the art of flying imprinted birds which are also used for breeding using artificial insemination (see page 101). To imprint a bird properly so that it does not scream and become a general pain in the arse, is incredibly time consuming, very messy (as it lives in the house with you to start with), easy to get wrong and personally I don't recommend it. There are few examples of what correct, total imprinting involves.

Some total imprint birds which have been imprinted sexually on purpose for artificial breeding, will only catch one item of quarry per day as they may not like the quarry to be removed from them. It is bad practice to upset imprints. This is, I imagine, possible to get over, and the bird could be asked to catch more per day once it has settled.

A friend of mine will not tail-bell his bird because he will not cast it (hold in the hands). This might upset his bird so much that it could take months to get over it, becoming frightened of the hand. When he told me this, I thought of how I cast some of my falcons here, if they have lost a bell or need a new jess in a hurry, and then fly them five minutes later. I really could not cope with having to pander to the whims of some blasted imprint. I happen to know that the person in question does not give his dog anywhere near that leeway.

A young bird to be imprinted has to be allowed to feed at all times, but must not see the handler provide the food, it must find the food itself. Once it is starting to get about, you must let it wander around and give it hours of your time, which is both very time consuming and disastrous to furniture if you have the bird in the house. The bird must be hooded at two to three weeks old and left to get used to it for longer periods each time. You cannot break a full grown imprint to the hood—it gets very upset and this breaks the bond of confidence.

An immature male European Goshawk, bred at The National Birds of Prey Centre

A total imprint has to be reared completely away from other birds, so really only one bird can be successfully imprinted each year, in one area, by one person. If the handler doesn't have the time and another member of the family is around more than he or she is, the bird may well imprint on them and even hate the sight of the original handler. It can take months to get an imprint to accept a different handler. Once the bird is full grown time must still be given to it daily, throughout the year, particularly coming up to the breeding season should it be required to produce either semen or eggs. Nor can the bird be left for more than a day during the breeding season, or it may switch off and take weeks to get going again.

There are many other techniques which have to be looked into before attempting to imprint a bird properly. I advise against it, although I am not really an expert on imprinting, having only done it on purpose twice. I suggest that anyone interested tries to get a copy of *Falcon Propagation* produced by The Peregrine Fund in the United States.

All in all, sexual imprints are very time consuming and no guarantee of captive breeding. Most of the breeding projects that were using large numbers of imprints to produce birds have, after several years, gone back to natural methods of breeding. I would far rather breed birds naturally than with artificial insemination. It is better for the birds, produces better young, is less time consuming and makes rearing 100 per cent easier. We do have two male falcons which will produce semen, but have never really used them properly. I have not flown imprints seriously, I don't want to, and most of my friends in Britain who have flown them would prefer not to again. I know a lot of American falconers fly imprinted birds and do it very well, perhaps they have the right temperament to cope with them and I don't.

There is, needless to say, the exception to the rule. Sparrowhawks are more fun, and appear to be more relaxed if imprinted. If you do it right they will still breed in the future. The call is a lovely noise, not at all offensive, and can be helpful as they will tell you when they are getting hungry and will call from a tree thus making it easier to locate them (see Sparrowhawk, Chapter 2). I have also found that the Black Sparrowhawk is easier to manage in this country if imprinted in a certain way.

Imprinting is a field about which we know relatively little. There are all sorts of types of imprinting. I have described some traits, and often they are unpleasant traits, which are found in the sexual imprint, as this is the bird that I consider the most difficult to cope with, apart from use as an artificial breeder.

European Eagle Owl (*Eric & David Hosking*)

So if you want to make sure of what you are getting—be careful and don't rush into things just because you are desperate to have a bird. When investing money in a new captive-bred bird, it has got to be worth giving the young creature the best chance to give *you* all the pleasure it can, and have a happy and useful life itself. The way to avoid most bad manners is to give all young birds time to grow up. We are all too keen to start immediately young birds are hard down and can be removed from the parents. It is far wiser and better in the long run to give young birds about one month, preferably on their own in a pen, before attempting to start training. It leads to a better behaved bird who is more balanced mentally, and will be more inclined to breed at a later date.

As many breeders are very pushed for space, they are unlikely to be able to remove the young from parents and house them in another pen until they are ready to leave for new owners. They are certainly unable to house each bird separately. This is why it is so vital to have a pen/weathering ground where a young bird can be put loose for at least two weeks, preferably four, before you start the training process. This will allow about four weeks for training during which any imprinting should show, thus keeping you within the guarantee time.

Whatever bird you have and whatever sort of place you build for it, the important thing to remember is—that creature relies on you, not only for its survival, but for its quality of life. It is up to any prospective owner to make sure that quality of life is what it should be. If you can't give a living creature the sort of care it deserves, then don't have the creature in the first place.

The Eagle Barn under construction

4 AVIARY BUILDING

Bearing in mind the fact that birds have to be ringed and registered; that the less disturbance the birds have, the better; the easier the pens are to manage the better; then the design of the aviary/pen is very important. We have been rebuilding since 1983 and still learn something new each time we put up a new block, because however hard we try, the pens always have something that we wish we had done differently in the long run. Apart from the fact that many of our old aviaries will fall down soon if we don't replace them, we have learnt a great deal about breeding birds since my father and mother first started The Falconry Centre. So we are building new pens to make life more pleasant and better for the birds, easier for us to manage with feeding, cleaning, breeding and ringing, but also trying to build something that blends in fairly well with the countryside.

We have tried to build for every extreme of weather conditions we have known over the last twenty years here—weight of snow up to two feet, gale force winds, freezing temperatures with very cold winds, high temperatures during droughts in summer (rare, I will admit) and most important in Britain, wet weather which needs good drainage. All these have been thought of; we have also tried to get away from quick building materials such as fence panels which, although speedy to erect, have a very short life span. I wonder now, after the hurricane force winds last year, how many people are wishing they had spent a little more on building. In the long run you get what you pay for. If you build cheaply you will regret it eventually.

If you have a choice, build pens facing west or south wherever possible, away from the freezing winds of winter. Part of the pen should always provide a sheltered area from the prevailing winds, so check from which direction your particular winds generally come. Light is vital to all species *including* owls. All birds love the first sunny days of spring. Light is important for both breeding, and healthy birds.

Much of what follows can be used as advice for building quarters for just one bird, used for flying, as well as for breeding pens. The same rules apply. Build well, with good materials to last. Don't cut corners or you will probably live to regret it. They are only suggestions and ideas taken from what we have built over the years, and experience gained over the last twenty-five.

We have always found that it is better and cheaper to start from scratch rather than try and adapt from something that was designed for a different job.

Our new pens have a block or brick wall, about 2ft (60cm) high above the ground and sometimes 3ft (90cm). The timber-framed pen is then placed on top of this. This gives several advantages. Firstly the timber lasts far longer. You can use standard size panels of weldmesh, if the front of the pen is to be open, and make any extra height in the pen with the wall. It helps against the invasion of vermin such as rats. It also looks nice, clean and professional and, if block work, the wall can be painted with an exterior paint. A bath can be built onto it easily.

Apart from the really nervous birds such as the *accipiters*, it is so much nicer if you can see your birds through a wire front, and it solves the problem of boredom which many species can suffer from, giving them something to look at. We have bred Peregrines, Harrises, Redtails, Ferruginous Buzzards, Blyth's Hawk Eagles, Kestrels, Redshouldered Buzzards, Caracaras, Egyptian Vultures and many Owls in open-fronted pens with many visitors looking on. We have even bred Goshawks in a wire-fronted pen, but not in front of visitors. As long as you place your pen sensibly and make sure that children, cars or dogs can't run up too close, there should be few problems. There will of course always be some pairs of birds that don't have the temperament to be in an open-fronted pen, and this will only be discovered by experience. But young birds put in for future breeding can be placed in open pens and settle well before getting to breeding age.

SIZE
Size of pen is something we are often asked about. Generally our rule of thumb is to build pens as spacious as we can afford. Birds can be bred in quite small pens, that has been proved many times. Being open to the public, we have a certain amount of pressure on us to give the birds as much room as possible. Anyway, I personally prefer to see our birds in good sized pens. The other thing you must remember is that a small pen may be okay for just the pair, but what sort of problems will you get if they raise six young for you? How dirty

will the pen get then? Will there be enough perches?—and so on.

The size will, however, depend on the birds you are building for. Our Eagle Barn is 27ft (8.2m) to the ridge, 17ft (7m) to the eaves; each pen is 15ft (4.5m) wide and 32ft (9.8m) long. The central service passage is 8ft (2.4m) wide and there is a lower and an upper one. Even then I should have liked to build bigger, but funds and space would not stretch any further. The next barn is for medium sized raptors such as Redtails, Goshawks, Harrises and similar sized birds. This will be 14ft (4m) to the eaves, 22ft (6.7m) to the ridge, with each pen 10ft (3m) wide and 20ft (6m) long. When you consider that each barn houses twelve pairs of birds, that starts to cover a fair amount of ground area. So as I will no doubt repeat many times thoughout this book: plan ahead, looking at what you hope to achieve in the future, so that you don't run out of space or have to build new pens in inaccessible places behind already existing ones. Suggested minimum pen sizes for birds appear on page 115.

Probably the most important aspect to think about with size of pens is height. The higher they are the more settled the birds will be. This means you have to be careful if you build a pen nice and high, to make it long enough for the birds to fly up and down without too much difficulty. High wing-loading birds such as Peregrines may land too heavily if the pen is very high but not long enough for the bird to reduce speed. So consider the birds you are building for and use your common sense.

FOUNDATIONS

As with any building, start with the foundations (which incidentally will probably be one of the most expensive parts of your pens), getting them dug and level and ready for building the wall. Remember to build the bath at this stage. Don't forget to leave a ground level space in the wall, for the door (you would be surprised how easy that is to forget—guess who's done it!).

BATHS

The baths we now use are built into the concrete block wall. We put a good foundation along the centre of the open front of the pen, or if a solid walled pen, in the centre of the wall nearest to water, and build out a square or rectangle, depending on the size of the birds who will require the bath. Don't forget to build it well away from the nest ledge or anywhere where droppings can foul the water. The rectangle is the same height as the wall and is almost filled with hardcore, the remaining few inches being lined with a mix of cement, making a shallow bath which can be flushed out with a hose. The wide 4in (10cm) sides of the concrete blocks are rounded off with the cement mix, making it comfortable for the birds to land on and good for their feet. The bottom may go green with algae, but if flushed out once a week the water stays remarkably clean. We put it in the centre of the wall to keep wings away from corners. Make sure that the concrete side closest to the woodwork is highest so that when it rains the water will overflow away from the timber. Also make sure that rainwater running off timber walls cannot wash any timber preservative into the bath. If put in a solid walled pen, drill a hole in the timber wall large enough to insert a hose and flush through the hole.

THE BASE
Next fill the pen with hardcore, the deeper the better. We put down about 9in (23cm) or more, giving less chance of rats, foxes or even one's own dog (could a falconer's dog possibly be that badly behaved?) digging through. The hardcore will drain the pen nicely and should stop any growth of greenery or weeds. We put a yearlong weed killer down before the hardcore. This kills everything for one year, and under the hardcore it cannot affect the birds. Tall growth of plant life in a pen causes problems, it hides vermin, keeps pens damp in wet spells, and small birds such as Little Owls or young birds just leaving the nest can get into tall wet growth and die of cold, unable to get out. On top of the hardcore we put large size gravel—1–3in (2.5–7.5cm). Smaller will just fall through the hardcore and be lost. Smaller gravel can be added on top if required. The whole result looks smart, is clean, drains excess water and can be maintained by hosing down regularly the soiled areas under perches and the like. For really heavy-landing birds such as big vultures, or Secretary Birds who spend a great deal of time walking, we put 6in (15cm) of sand on the top. You will notice that the perches are not in yet. Although this means that some of the base will have to be moved, this is easier than trying to build round perches that catch on everything and are a pain. Leave them until last when the front is put into position. The exception is if you like the idea of the made-up trees as perches (see page 113) get the pine poles in before the hardcore.

FRAMING
The size of the timber used varies, depending on the size of the structure and the roof it has to support. We are now using CLS which is a stress graded timber, but we are building pretty large barns. For most people 4in×2in (10cm×5cm) treated timber should be fine. This goes up onto the wall, remembering to put a damp proof course (DPC) on first, and will cheer you up as it should go up quickly. All our new pens have either a central passage or a passage running along the back. This is for servicing, cleaning, feeding, monitoring, etc. Make it wide enough to get a wheelbarrow down easily, preferably leaving

the skin on your knuckles. Remember this building should last you at least twenty years; build it pleasant to work with.

The door to the pen should be from the passage. Don't make it three foot square and have to climb over a bath to get in. Build it for human height and wide enough for the wheelbarrow to turn into the pen, 6ft 6in×3ft 6in (2m×1m) is fine. In that way you will not brain yourself regularly. It is opening into a dark passage so you need not worry about escapes. In our Eagle Barn the doors open inwards. The nest ledge and feed ledge should also be on the passage wall. You can then enter without fear of losing the bird, watching becomes easier, feeding is done without young seeing you produce the food, eggs can be taken and young replaced with slightly less hazard, and your security should also be improved.

We generally use a material called sterling board (9 or 12mm) to clad the framing, but we have a solid roof on most of our pens so they are protected from the weather. We also use $^1/_2$in (1.25cm) feather boarding 6in (15cm) wide and treated, or exterior grade plywood, or 6in×1in (15cm×2.5cm) end boarding. The passage is clad with a smooth surface using sterling board, so doors work properly, and fixing for nest and feed ledges becomes easier. The front of the pen is covered with boarding if you are building a solid walled pen or with twilweld or weldmesh or similar if the pen is to be open-fronted; 2in (5cm) mesh is fine for most birds except American Kestrels, Little Owls or smaller birds.

ROOFING

Since starting to write this we have completed the building of our Eagle Barn and Barn No 2, and I am now in no doubt about roofing. These new buildings are completely roofed over with plastic-coated steel sheets and large areas of roof lights. Some of our other pens have a netting roofing with shelter over the nest ledges. I prefer the totally roofed pens as it solves far more problems than it creates, and makes building easier and more structurally sound. The advantages are that the pen is warmer and safer for the parent birds, and you can sit safely in your house watching the pouring rain or falling snow knowing that however silly your birds are they cannot sit out getting soaked and cold. The same applies with young that have just left the nest. The food will always stay dry and not get dropped into snow by birds and then lost. If the perching is correctly placed, the birds can get plenty of sun during one end of the day or the other. If they really want to get wet then they can usually sit in what rain may be driven in on a windy day. There is also less chance of weeds growing.

The disadvantages are that the rain does not wash droppings away so you have to do that, and possibly in continuous dry weather the pen may get dusty, either from nest ledge material or dust and feather remains from plucked food. This could possibly cause asperiglosis. However, as those weather conditions are far rarer than damp weather, we are going for total roof coverage. A quick spray with a hose will lay the dust.

Needless to say, if the roof is totally covered, the front must be wire to allow for plenty of fresh air and a vent or wooden louver in the back wall of each pen will give through ventilation. In very cold weather there is condensation as the sun warms the cold roof. So far this has not seemed to worry the birds. It is a solvable problem, using under-roof insulation, which is an option we may take at a later date.

When building an open roof with one end sheltered, we use a $1^1/_2$in (4cm) mesh nylon net as covering. It is made to measure by Bridport Gundrey Netting. The important thing about any net is the thickness of the individual strands. This netting is similar to tennis-court netting and the strands are about $^1/_8$in (3mm) thick. This means that the birds cannot cut themselves if they fly into it, and should not be able to twist the net around their toes and injure themselves. It is also very strong, very quick to put up, very light and, over a reasonable span supported with high - tension wire it should support an average weight of snow, although in heavy falls snow should be knocked off. We rebuilt one of our owl blocks with this netting as the roofing material and promptly came across the only problem that we have encountered with it—rats. If they can climb the wall to the roof they seem to love eating through it, leaving holes large enough for birds to escape. We solved this problem by

The finished Eagle Barn

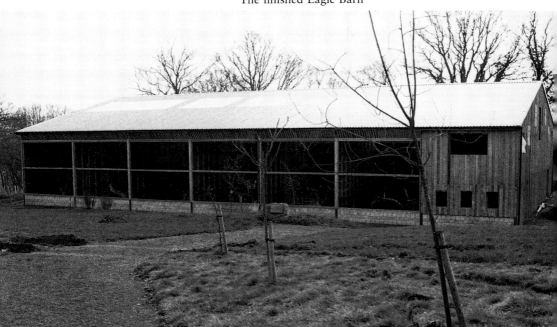

Some pens for very tame owls, with a nylon netting roof

putting 1in (2.5cm) wire netting on top. This was fine for the owls who tend not to fly up to the roof, but would not be good for birds that are inclined to be roof climbers or hitters. This is yet another good reason for having a solid roof. A friend of mine came across an interesting problem with plastic-coated chain link, which you would think would be really good apart from needing strong support. He found one of his birds with wing feathers caught in the overlap of the chain link and having hung for some time before he found it. So, if wire is to be used, you can only go for thick-gauge welded mesh and even that will damage birds if they hit it hard with either feet or tops of heads. Netlon, a plastic windbreak material, is quite good to put beneath wire mesh roofs as long as you use the thick gauge. Remember that *any* thin gauge material, be it plastic, nylon, wire or whatever will cut birds. So if we were going for uncovered roofs we would make sure that no vermin could climb to the roof and we would use thick stranded nylon mesh.

SHELTER

Many of our old pens have just small areas covered to give birds protection. Some people cover only one or two corners; I don't think this is enough. It is not sufficient to shelter birds from driving rain or snow, nor does it give them the chance to move about in the sheltered area. You may find that pairs will not roost together, so, if there is little shelter only the dominant bird will use it and the other may be out in all weathers. This may not harm the bird, but continual *surviving*

A smaller roofed set of pens

of bad weather conditions is unnecessary, and may well shorten the bird's life. Certainly, nest ledges should be very well covered so that no driving rain can enter. Feed ledges should also be covered. There is hardly anything more worrying than seeing food drop into deep snow in the pens, and even if the snow is moved how does one know that the birds haven't lost some of their rations? All this increases my delight in the fact that our new pens are totally covered so that I don't have to worry about these problems. If you are going for partially sheltered pens then cover the whole of one end up to half the length of the pen. If you use light-giving panels (translucent plastic types) then you can allow plenty of light into nest areas without minimising the sheltered area. Remember though that excessive heat can also cause problems so don't put your light-giving panels directly over the nest ledge. There are now available plastic sheets that are double glazed to solve the problem of a heat build-up.

For shelter-building materials use good-sized timbers for strength and support. Our Eagle Barn roofing material is plastic-coated steel sheeting, with plenty of transparent roof lights inserted to allow sunlight into the pen. We tested the temperature in the pens last summer while building and are not worried about overheating. If we do by any chance get a very hot summer we can insulate the undersurface with no problems. Do not use asbestos as it is a dangerous material, but several types of concrete-based roofing sheets are very good and solve any heat problem. They are, however, very heavy and so need considerable support. My stables are roofed in

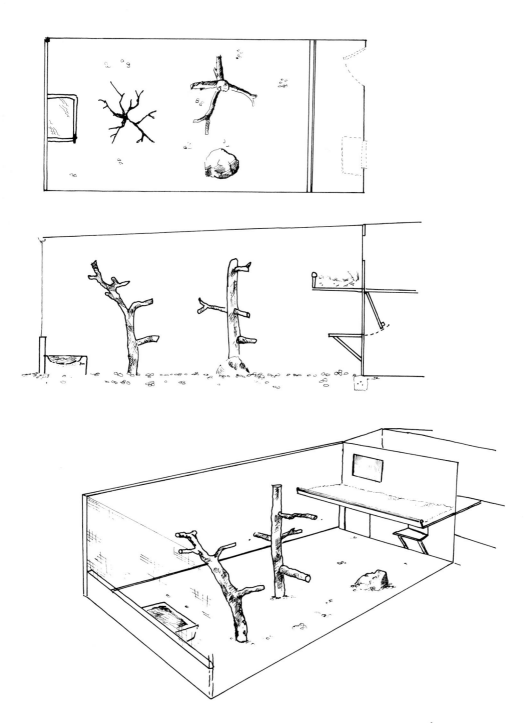

The aviary, showing perches, nest and food ledges, the bath and the sheltered area

a product called Onduline. This is a very attractive material, seems to insulate reasonably, lasts well and I like it very much. It is only affected with condensation in freezing conditions. However it does need more support than other materials and should be fixed on every ridge at the front.

Whatever you do about roofing, don't forget to put up good strong gutters. These are vital and will keep your pen much drier. Dig a good deep soakaway well outside the pen for the roof water to drain away.

NEST LEDGES

Throw away all nests using old car tyres. They harbour disease and insects and, in my opinion have no place in a breeding pen. Make all nest ledges as big as possible. The Eagle Barn ledges are 8ft (2.4m) wide, 15ft (4.5m) long, with a lip of 9in (23cm); the ledges in the pens for Redtails, Peregrines and the like are 4ft (1.2m) wide by 10ft(3m)long, and all nest ledges have the same 9in(23cm) lip. This

Nest ledges

length of ledge, running right across the back of the pen, is designed to be part of the structure. The supports go right across the central passage and into the pens on either side, giving the nest ledges support, and support for an upper passage for viewing. The long ledge gives the birds a limited choice of nest area ie they can choose one end or the other but still be in the area we need them in for monitoring. But even more important, it is to give babies room to spread out when they are starting to fledge, particularly if you have asked the parents to rear a good number of young. If you don't give growing eyasses plenty of room you will find that young get very dirty, and they may push one another out of the nest before they are ready to leave it. A large nest ledge avoids this and the possible resulting injury.

The lip should be high enough for you to put down a good depth of peat, pea gravel or sand and still leave the babies enough height to stop them falling out during the early stages. We put down a base of one or other of the above materials in all the nest ledges, even with nest-building birds. We have found that if the birds build a poor nest the eggs can slip through, and if they land on hard timber they don't last long. If they have a soft landing they should be all right. **Note**: Always use a coarse Irish moss peat, not the fine black peat, and mix it with pea gravel. Fine peat kills hatching eggs and young.

All nest ledges should be cleared, cleaned and disinfected before *each* breeding season. Bacteria will undoubtedly build up. If you don't clean them regularly, after a while infection is bound to get into eggs.

PERCHES

I don't like to see perches nailed across corners of pens. The walls get dirty and the wooden perches season over the years, getting very hard. This can cause foot damage. *Ninety-nine per cent of bumblefoot is caused by poor perches.*

We have access to a number of trees, many of which need pruning at intervals, so we choose well-shaped large branches and dig them into the ground giving the effect of a tree with several perching places. These work well and look nice. If placed sensibly the walls of the pens need not get fouled, and they make excellent perches for young just learning to branch. With the Eagle Barn it was difficult to find trees large enough and even when we did they were almost impossible to manage; so we bought twelve tall poles of pine from the local woods. The diameter was about 12in (30cm), even these were pretty impossible to manage and had to go in before the roof went on. Then using a small chain saw (don't use one if you are not experienced, find someone who will give you a hand for they are very dangerous machines) we cut mortices (square holes) in several places in the poles, we then cut tenons on the ends of various branches we had collected, and fitted them into the holes, giving us a hand–made tree with branches in all the right places. With a little imagination they can look great and are very effective even if it is a little odd to see oak branches on a pine trunk.

Avoid fruit-tree timber if you can. Once the bark comes off with time, the timber underneath has nasty and very sharp points which are not good for the birds' feet. Oak, beech, elder or elm are good. If you plant willow branches in the ground, remember they will probably grow.

Don't forget to have at least one perch large enough to hold a pair of mating birds comfortably. After all who wants to mate in discomfort? Perches near the nest ledge are vital for young to grab at should they slip, and for them to land on either to leave or return to the nest.

We have just added a new perch in the Eagle Barn as we did not have enough perches near the wire. If you have a really good high perch wire, then birds are far less likely to hit the front. So we put in what we call budgie bars. We thought they might not work and everyone was very sceptical, but they are a great success and the birds love them. Get a decent sized branch, one-third the length of the width of the pen. Put a rope round each end leaving two equal lengths free at each end of the perch for tying at the height you require. Attach to the purlins and, hey presto, a budgie bar. It tends to swing from side to side rather than front to back, and thus exercises the bird.

FOOD LEDGES

These are placed under the nest ledges, backing onto the service passage for access. Food ledges placed under the nest ledge tend to discourage the birds feeding there, as they prefer high perches generally. This should keep the feed ledge much cleaner. The ledge can be washed down from the service passage without disturbing young as they can't see you. Get adult birds used to all maintenance processes well before the breeding season. The feed ledge being under the nest ledge also gives the adults a little more work to do in getting food to the young which is no bad thing, especially for the male.

The other very important reason for this placement of the feed ledge is that at no time can young see you bringing food. Young Harris Hawks, even though parent reared, will associate humans with food later in life if they see them bring food each day. With the feed ledge below the nest ledge, they see the food only when it arrives with the parent bird, thus ensuring no imprint tendencies and producing, in my opinion, nicer birds to handle if being flown.

As stated before, the food ledge should be sheltered from rain and snow to keep food pleasant for birds and visible. It should also be kept as clean as possible at all times.

OTHER POSSIBILITIES

If you can afford it, before the pens are finished run power to them. To be able to turn on safe, outside lights is wonderful on dark winter nights, should you be worried about the birds. Perhaps for some reason they haven't been fed during daylight hours, or something has disturbed them and you are afraid that they won't get up to their perches. There are many reasons and you will never regret the expense. It will also help from the security point of view.

A tip in bad weather which I learnt from Jim Weaver when I visited the Peregrine Fund at Ithaca in the United States. They have pretty cold winters over there and they also have total covered roofing. When the weather is bad, they tack up a large plastic sheet (translucent builder's plastic is fine) with battens onto the front of the pen. It makes the pen much snugger for really cold spells, is easy to store for re-use, and is cheap and quick to install. If you are worried about circulation of fresh air, leave a small gap at the top.

OUTSIDE THE PEN

As running lawn-mowers and such like close to breeding pens is not a good idea, a strip of gravel on a hardcore base round the outside of the pens, about 3ft (1m) wide, will keep pens cleaner, tidier and more secure. The birds will always know you are there anyway, so don't worry about the noise when you walk on it.

SOME SUGGESTED MINIMUM PEN SIZES

Large eagles and vultures	30ft long×15ft wide×16ft high (9×4.5×4.8m)
Buzzards, large falcons, eagle owls, small eagles small vultures, large hawks	20ft long×10ft wide×12ft high (6×3×3.6m)
Small falcons, small hawks, small owls	12ft long×8ft wide×8ft high (3.6×2.4×2.4m)
Tiny owls and falcons	10ft long×10ft wide×8ft high (3×3×2.4m)

Young Prairie Falcon

5 CAPTIVE BREEDING

There can be no doubt now that the future of falconry and keeping raptors lies in captive breeding. Having said that, however, I believe strongly that anyone wanting to breed birds of prey should think very hard about it before starting. There are so many different factors to consider. Breeding raptors is not cheap. The birds themselves are expensive, sensibly built pens even more so. If you want to get involved with artificial incubation, then incubators, brooders, the rooms to house them and the electricity to run them can easily run into thousands of pounds—to say nothing of the enormous amount of time required.

It has been stated, even recently in print, in at least two countries to my knowledge, that it is not possible to breed birds of prey, particularly Peregrines, in captivity. I find it very difficult to believe anyone is stupid enough to come out with such rubbish. Should any of these doubting Thomases care to come and stay here, they will see us produce a number of Peregrines perfectly genuinely each year. I believe I could put these people, who suffer from a lack of research before printing, lack of experience and lack of brains, to good use as vulture food.

There are various ways in which to go about captive breeding. These can be divided into groups according to ease and cost effectiveness; although if you are into cutting corners don't try to breed birds of prey as you will probably fail. The most important fact to remember is that whatever you produce and for whatever reason, the birds should be needed, either by people, or for good conservation reasons. They should be of good quality and, if leaving your care, have the chance of belonging to someone who will care for them well.

Over the years a number of people have come to us and shown an interest in captive breeding. They usually say that they want to start with Kestrels or Tawny Owls. Now although I have nothing against Kestrels—indeed, they are lovely birds with great character, excellent flyers in the wild, and beautiful to watch hovering in their natural environment—they do not make particularly good falconry birds and are definitely not ideal for beginners. They are small, weigh very little, can be very easy to kill through lack of experience and so generally have a limited market to go to, should you breed them.

When I ask would-be breeders what they are going to do if they are successful and breed young, many haven't thought that far ahead. When you consider that it is possible to breed up to six or even seven young Kestrels a year, that is a fairly large number of young to deal with responsibly, and the numbers soon add up. Some potential breeders suggest they intend releasing the young back to the wild. Kestrels are our commonest diurnal raptor. At the moment they don't need replenishing in the wild. In places where they have declined there is a reason for it. If young Kestrels are released into an area where wild Kestrels already exist, the chances are that they will either be driven away by the resident birds and eventually die or they may, if successful, drive out the wild pairs that should be there. Either solution is not a good one and the birds should not be released. If an area has no Kestrels, it is most likely because the area is unsuitable for some reason, and unless you know that reason and can solve it, released Kestrels will either disperse onto other Kestrels' territories or die. Most of the above could also be said of Tawny Owls.

So generally speaking, it is not a good idea to release raptors of any species until a great deal of groundwork has been done. The birds should be needed in the wild and the situation should be right for release schemes. It is vital to try to breed birds that can have a use in one way or another and thus the individual birds will have the chance of a happy life. If you look at the breeding of dogs in this country you have a classic example of what I am trying to explain. Far too many dogs are bred, often it is very difficult to find good homes for them. Tens of thousands are destroyed every year because there is no use for them, no one wants them. This is heartbreaking, a criminal waste of life and totally the fault of irresponsible humans. Although that situation has not yet been reached with raptors, we must be aware of it *before* it happens. There are many species of raptors which would benefit from more attempts at captive breeding, so if you are interested in doing this, choose species that can be useful.

One would think that the easiest way of breeding raptors is to put a pair together and leave it to them to produce young and rear them for you. Sound easy, doesn't it? I wish it was.

Firstly the pair have to be compatible. Secondly, with the true *accipiters* such as Goshawks, those people breeding them regularly have found that they do much better if kept apart for most of the year, which means two pens not one, and considerable amounts of

Baby Harris Hawks

watching time to see *if* and when they are ready to go together for breeding. Parent birds of prey may not sit the eggs well, either deserting or breaking them. They may decide to desert, or even eat the young. If care is not taken, there are many problems that can beset the young before they are ready to leave the nest. Then just to make life easy, all the young produced, unless they are Owls, Vultures or Secretary Birds, have to be close rung with government rings; this in itself can cause problems when having to go into pens to ring young. So, as you can see, even the easiest way of trying to breed birds has many problems to be solved before success is gained.

Never discount the amount of time, effort and money captive breeding is going to cost you. If you are hoping to make vast amounts of money at it, my advice is don't bother. If you take into account the hours you spend, plus all the capital outlay, by the time you have reasonable numbers of birds producing the price will probably have dropped and you will end up earning an hourly rate that will horrify you. If on the other hand all you want to do is produce a few birds each year either from a breeding pair, or even using your flying birds, then just build very good pens and don't go in for all the intricacies and expense of double clutching, incubating and all the rest of the palaver. Let the birds get on with it. It does work if you can get it right, and there are various less expensive techniques to help the birds learn how to rear young safely and well. Sort out the techniques and requirements that will suit what you want to do; this chapter will, I hope, help. If you want to breed large numbers, seriously, be prepared to spend a lot of money to get things right. I do, all the time!

What should always be borne in mind is the reason you are breeding the birds. Are they for falconry or for further captive breeding and if so, to what end? Are they for zoos or for release programmes? All this will dictate the quality and type of young to be produced. If falconers can become self-sufficient in birds, other than occasionally needing a fresh input of genetic stock from the wild, which could be exchanged with captive-bred stock, then falconry will have a better chance of surviving. Please note that I only say 'better', as the increasing forces against falconry and indeed any livestock in captivity, such as animal liberation movements and many other organisations, should never be discounted.

The NBoP Centre has produced 42 species of young so far, and normally rears between 80 and 100 young a year. We have probably made many of the mistakes there are to be made. The important thing is to learn by one's mistakes and never think that you know all there is to know; always keep an open mind and don't be afraid to admit mistakes. Common sense is a very valuable aid to managing any life form, sadly it is becoming rare, verging on the extinct.

The following headings used in this chapter should be useful in the production of good quality birds, which we at the Centre try very hard to do:

Baby Sparrowhawk

●Quality of Young Produced
●Time Available for Rearing
●Possible Number of Young
●Natural Hatch and Rear
●Double Clutching
●Incubation
●Rearing Facilities
●Food and Supplements
●Feeding Young Birds
●Returning Young
●Aviary Space
●Problems
●Disposal of Surplus Birds

These may not cover every aspect needed, but many problems can usually be thought out if common sense is used. In emergencies The Falconry Centre is on the end of the phone. Please be civilised about the time you phone however.

Quality of Young Produced

The first thing to be considered is what type of young you wish to produce. Here, one hopes, some sort of moral consideration comes into play. It would be very easy to remove all eggs from laying pairs, egg pull (take each egg as it is laid), triple or perhaps quadruple clutch, hand rear all the young right the way up to adulthood and sell them to any and all comers. This is very bad policy, for the following reasons;

1 As many of those producing birds will be falconers, it is bad for the sport of falconry. This sort of behaviour makes breeders seem greedy, uncaring, and thus does us no good in the public eye, the opinion of vets in the know, nor in the eyes of conservation bodies.

2 I believe *over* clutching and pulling is bad for the producing pair. It can very easily overtax the laying female and often doesn't give the pair the chance to finish the cycle by rearing young—incidentally weakening the pair bond and decreasing the chances of future breeding because they are not allowed to finish the natural process. So why risk the goose that lays the golden egg, as it were?

3 So often at The NBoP Centre, unfortunate people come to us who have bought a bird without doing their homework, and have ended up with an imprint, which they don't want and don't know how to cope with. It is usually the worst sort of imprint that will not be

of use either for natural breeding or artificial insemination and is a pain in the arse for falconry purposes.

4 Worst of all, this form of greed is very bad for the young produced. Many of them end up being birds that no one wants, going from owner to owner on a downward scale until some unsuspecting and uninformed person buys the bird because the price is low, and then he or she kills it through inexperience. This is shameful for all of us and is largely the responsibility of the original breeder.

Time Available for Rearing

As already mentioned, what should be realised before any hand rearing is attempted, is that it is very time-consuming. Food has to be prepared daily—large numbers of young go through vast quantities of food. Hygiene takes time, and the process of feeding is not fast, particularly with the odd awkward baby making life infuriatingly slow. We can spend up to seven hours a day preparing food and feeding young in the height of the season. Even one baby can take over an hour a day and, unluckily for those people with other jobs, the young need to be cared for throughout the day. Just to really cheer you up, even more time is needed if things go wrong and you have a sick baby to care for. So bear the time element heavily in mind before deciding on your breeding plan.

In my opinion, there are only two ways to rear young birds of prey, to give well adjusted, pleasant adults. One is to let the birds get on with the whole thing ie parent-hatched and reared birds, only giving you one clutch. I had to do this with my Prairie Falcon last year and she hatched and reared four lovely young for me, even taking on four other young falcons when her own young were three weeks old. What more could one ask? The other way, which will increase production, is to hand rear the first clutch until the young can be ringed and then return them to parents or foster parents. This should then give you a second clutch which can be left to the parents if the first clutch is fostered to other rearing birds in the same family group. If you have a very good pair of proven rearing parent birds, and well constructed pens, the first clutch can be returned to the parent birds and the second clutch can join them later. This will depend very much on the species involved and the gap between the clutches.

Egg pulling is also possible, but it makes rearing the young very much more difficult. It is not particularly good for the adults, some birds will not respond to it, and I don't really recommend it (see page 120).

The deciding factor for which method is used will be time—the availability of someone, good with birds, being close by hand-reared young at all times during the rearing period for care and feeding, in case of problems with young, power cuts or faulty equipment. There seems to be little point in having alarm systems for equipment unless there is someone there to hear them. If there is no one available, natural hatch and rearing is the only other alternative for most people.

There is one other option. A few people breeding from their birds, work in conjunction with The NBoP Centre. These are people we know and trust. Eggs are brought here and we do much of the work of hatching and rearing first and second clutches, using our birds as fosters and our pens to keep the young safe. This is not a free service—even to our friends, I am afraid—as the costs are high. We have a minimum of a quarter of the young, if the parent birds are not ours, and more if either parent belongs to the Centre. If anyone wants to enter into that sort of contract with other breeders or friends, make sure that everyone knows what the rules are. In that way, friends are not lost through misunderstandings.

The Department of the Environment (DoE) must be informed if eggs or young are moving from one person to another. Strict records should be kept at all times.

Possible Numbers of Young

As you should know what possible breeding pairs you have at the start of the breeding season, you should plan the season accordingly, asking yourself the following questions.

• Are you going to leave the birds to hatch and rear?
• Are you going to double clutch?
• Are you going to egg pull?
• What number of eggs are possible?
• What is the maximum number of young likely?
• What possible pairs are available for rearing?
• What spare aviary space have you, available for young?
• Is there a responsible market for the species you may produce?

You need to know these points because it will affect plans for rearing facilities, the time available for rearing, the quarters needed for growing young, and the quantities of food that may be required. So plan ahead.

Should you only wish to produce enough young for your own and friends' use, without the quite considerable expense of double clutching and/or hand rearing and all that goes with it, leave the birds to it after checking that your eggs are fertile. If they are fertile, leave the whole process to the parents. Provide plenty of food once the young have hatched, increasing the quantity as they grow, and feeding at least twice a day and preferably more.

Should you, however, wish to produce a larger number of young so that you have birds of your own and can either give away, or defray some of the costs by the selling of surplus, a great deal more work, money and time has to be spent. Many people who want to double clutch and incubate eggs tend to think far more about the incubation aspects than the rearing of young. As I think incubation is generally far harder than rearing young, this is fair enough. However, eggs do not take up a great deal of room, or time, and don't shit everywhere either, so there are many things to consider if larger numbers are required.

Natural Hatch and Rear

This is the most nerve-wracking method, especially for inexperienced breeders, as it appears that so many things can go wrong. However, when it goes well, it is definitely the most satisfying of the lot. Added to that, the young should turn out to be the best adjusted birds and more likely to breed themselves in the future. Basically all you do is provide the best pen, nest ledge, food, nesting material (if they are nest builders), and give the birds time and peace. Only check on them when you need to, not every ten minutes of the day because you want to know what is going on.

Watch when the birds start to lay and record anything like mating, food passing and the like. Watch when they start to sit tight and watch for the first young to hatch. It's all very exciting, but the less disturbance the better, particularly with first-time parents. You should only need to upset the birds for the ringing of the young and if you time it well that should not be too traumatic for either the young or the adults.

There is only one management technique that can be very useful with natural hatch and rear. That is to check the fertility of the clutch of eggs, particularly with first-time layers. Don't do this until the birds have been sitting fairly tight for ten days. Collect the eggs from the nest ledge during the morning, in daylight. This will give parent birds time to settle and get back onto eggs. Choose a day that is not too cold or wet if you can. Of course if you have totally roofed pens the wet doesn't matter! Remove the eggs, leaving the same number of warm hens' eggs. Take them to a dark safe room and candle them ie look through them with a strong light to test for fertility. If the eggs are fertile, put them straight back under the parents, if they are not, remove the dummy hens' eggs immediately. Then, if the birds recycle, there may be a chance of a fertile second clutch. If they do not, at least you have had a good try and lost nothing. If some of the eggs look fertile then return all of them, the others may just not be as developed.

We have an American candler made by Lyon Electric Co Inc. It works very well and there are few eggs that I cannot candle with it. Some people use a 40 watt light bulb mounted (in its holder) on a piece of wood with a coffee tin over the top and sponge on top of that so that the egg is cushioned and the light focussed through the hole in the top. Do not move the egg round violently, and do not leave it in one position too long or you may cook it.

Removing infertile first clutches does not increase production. Some birds may lay one less egg in the second clutch, but as long as that second clutch is fertile I don't suppose you will mind.

It is a good idea to learn what a fertile egg looks like. I have nearly thrown away eggs that were in fact fertile. (See the Bibliography for further information on eggs.) Ten days' incubation should show fertility easily, with the possible exception of very thick-shelled eggs such as Ferruginous, Redtails or some eagles. If you are experienced, candle them at seven days from the parent bird starting to sit seriously. If the parent birds have been very obvious with their mating, then there should be no need to check for fertility.

The risk with natural hatch and rear is in the parents failing to rear the young. Once the adults have proved that they will rear young

Candling an egg

without mishap and you have provided all they need to do the job well, then all you have to do is sit back and wait for the time when the young are ready to remove. If the birds have not reared before, you will not know how successful they can be. Most birds, if you leave them to it and don't constantly disturb them, should manage—especially if you help a little with such things as skinning the food and giving it little and often to stimulate the adults into feeding the young. If however you keep disturbing them and drooling over the young there is little chance of them getting it right. Unless you give them a try the first year, you will not know if things are going to go wrong.

We give all laying birds the chance to rear young, regardless of whether or not their eggs are fertile. We have the advantage of large numbers of young to hand round to parents and we are always needing foster parents. We nearly always stick to the same family group, ie falcons with falcons, hawks with hawks, and we have switched buzzards and eagles as they are very closely related. This means that even before we are getting fertile eggs from some pairs, they are proven rearers. It strengthens the pair bond, sometimes producing fertile eggs the following year. If you have other birds producing, or can borrow young from friends, this is a first-class way to bring parents on.

There is a risk, but you have to take that risk to get parent-reared birds. However I feel very strongly that it is worth the risk to be able to produce nicely behaved, well-mannered, mentally stable birds. (See Returning Young below for further information.)

Double Clutching

We double clutch most of our birds. It makes it easier on the parents and does not cause great problems when trying to return young to parents or foster parents. As two of our pairs of Harris Hawks have naturally triple clutched, we sometimes ask just the Harrises to triple clutch under more controllable circumstances, rather than leave it to them and suddenly get late August clutches.

Most of the clutches are removed after a week of natural incubation and put into the incubators. If we require the parents to double clutch we leave them with no eggs. If we do not require more eggs, but want to put young back, we leave them with hens' eggs to keep them sitting. Sometimes when parents have not recycled and we have young to return, we put in hens' eggs to see if they will sit again. This often works, and once the birds have been sitting tight for a few days, the dummy eggs can be removed and young put in to replace them.

All these plans are made well before the breeding season, taking into consideration the performance of the pairs in the previous year. Once a particular plan has been made, we try to stick to it rather than mess the birds around and end up with nothing and, more importantly, no knowledge gained of their behaviour.

Eggs are removed with the greatest of care and more than one person will be needed if the adult birds are aggressive. Apart from being careful about your face when going into pens with aggressive birds, forget the rest of you; it will heal and probably doesn't show anyway. The most important concern should be the eggs. Some females will fiercely protect the nest regardless of the damage done to the eggs; this is one of the reasons we suggest a deep nest ledge covering. If she is aggressive, the female should be caught up first, as quickly as possible, to minimise egg damage. Get someone to hold on to her until the eggs have been collected. Males tend to do no egg damage although some will attack the intruding humans.

If the pair are not aggressive and just leave the nest area, then get on with the job quickly and leave. But always watch the birds. They will often wait until you lose eye-contact for a while and then hit you. Some pairs may even be really organised; one bird will go for the intruder, and while the latter turns to face the oncoming bird, the other will have a go from behind. Be cheerful though; if they are this protective it shows they consider the pen belongs to them which is great.

Place the eggs in clean cotton wool in a box making sure they do not touch one another, and take to the incubators as quickly as possible. Do not shake or jostle them. Bumping around will cause more egg damage than chilling. Release the female on leaving the pen. Have clean hands when collecting eggs and the box and cotton wool should also be clean.

It is a very sensible idea to keep good records on eggs and young. I am not as good at this as I should be, but I am trying to improve. Not only are such records very valuable to refer to for laying dates, past performance and so on, but with the current legislation it is very important to document all breeding attempts. To keep brief records the year round will help you to be in practice for the breeding season, and over the years will give you far greater knowledge of your birds.

Incubation

Almost everyone who is breeding birds seriously has found that their hatch success rate is considerably higher if the eggs get a week to ten days of natural incubation prior to going into artificial incubators. However there will be times when it is not possible to leave the eggs with the parent birds. One reason is the weather. If the pair lay early, when frosts are still likely, it can be dangerous to leave the eggs with them, particularly if they are ground-nesting birds such as some of the owls. The eggs can get frosted in a very short time.

Lanner

The 'girls'—free range

The second reason is that a few birds may tend to foul their eggs badly. We have a pair of Lanners who make their eggs filthy very quickly. In this case we remove the eggs as they are laid, replacing each one with a dummy egg and the real eggs are incubated in the incubators from day one.

We have tried, over the last few years, hatching a number of eggs by artificial incubation from day one, and although we hatch some I am sure we would be much more successful if we didn't have to do this. To this effect we are trying hens as natural incubators this coming season. We got the hens last August and they are now used to us and fairly tame. They have just started to lay and we shall let some of them go broody. I am keeping them in a free-range condition (praying the flying demonstration birds don't decide to eat them). Once they have gone broody each bird will be moved to a secure indoor area where the whole process can be monitored and kept scrupulously clean. Keeping them outside until they go broody is nicer for the hens and makes them easier to manage and keep clean.

The hens must be got used to handling so that we can place and remove raptor eggs safely. It is best to see how well each hen will sit before risking valuable eggs. Once the eggs have had a week to ten days' natural incubation, under whatever bird used, they will then be moved into the incubator room.

We are lucky enough to have a separate room for incubation. This is kept clean at all times and the incubators sit on very sturdy surfaces, so they cannot be knocked. The room is off-bounds to all during the breeding season to avoid incubators being jarred or turned off while the vacuum cleaner is being used. Anyone wanting to come in always knocks first to avoid eggs at risk.

Sensibly, the incubator room, like the brooder room, should be kept at a constant temperature, making it much easier for the incubators to remain at a constant heat internally. Make sure that no sunlight can touch any incubator as this will overheat it and kill the eggs. We have a kitchen-type blind over the one window and it is drawn throughout the breeding season. We can then darken the room with a second black-out curtain for candling.

We use Roll–X incubators and have seven of them. Six will be in use during the height of the season with the seventh as a standby incubator. The reason we use Roll–X is that parts are easy to get, the eggs can be seen without opening the top, they are easy to clean and generally very reliable. We do change the temperature control knob from the one provided (which is not very good to use), to a ten–turn potentiometer which is far better.

Whatever we use, I would always stick to all the incubators being the same make rather than having one of one make and one of another. For maintenance and care it is far more sensible to stick to one variety only. When you first get an incubator it is a good idea

The incubator room at The Falconry Centre

Jo with the Roll-X incubator. Notice how the Netlon is placed between the two grids and supports the smaller owl and falcon eggs

to take it to bits and put it together again. In this way you will get to know it, be able to fix minor problems in emergencies and not be afraid of it. The Roll—X is easy to understand and even I can dismantle and assemble one.

We don't place our eggs sharp end down, in the holes provided on the various grids. It doesn't seem very natural to me and there have been cases where the eggs have been broken. We place the eggs on their sides. As we have a large size difference in the eggs we are hatching, we place a piece of plastic Netlon, the same material as is used in the pens for nervous birds, in the incubator. The material is cut to fit between the two grids and the incubator works as normal apart from the addition of, essentially, a third grid. The Netlon is softish, all the edges are rounded, it is easy to cut and easy to keep clean. Not even the Pygmy Falcon eggs will fall through as the holes are less than $1/4$in (6mm) in diameter.

Once you have incubators, and you will need at least three for serious breeding, set them up where they will normally be kept, and run them. Throw away any cheap thermometers that tend to come with incubators and get good ones. Test all of them before use—put them into a bowl with ice to bring them all down and then place in warm water. It is unlikely that all will read the same but any that are way out should be returned. We use Zeal's thermometers and we put at least five in each incubator. All incubators have hot spots; by running the incubator well in advance of the breeding season, these spots can be marked out by moving thermometers around the incubator.

Your incubator will only be as good as the equipment used for measuring temperature and humidity. I have to admit that I have not been impressed by instruments to measure the latter. Unless you spend a great deal of money, most of them are pretty unreliable after a short time, and the expensive ones are not designed for small systems like ours. However, hairline hygrometers will give you a per cent reading and should remain fairly accurate if adjusted very regularly.

All incubators should be run and tested for some time before raptor eggs are placed in them. Run the spare before the season starts, to check it is okay. If you have not incubated eggs before, it is only sense to run a batch of chicken eggs through and hatch them well before the breeding season to get some practice, and give you confidence in the incubators.

We run our incubators at 99°F (37°C) and unless the weather is very dry for an extended period we place no water in them. Having measured the humidity in my incubator room, it rarely drops below 50 per cent and that means that the incubators should have enough humidity. I throw away most of the Roll−X water fountains, they are pretty useless, and if putting in any water we use 3in (7cm) petri dishes. I still use the fountain in the hatching incubator, which has water in it at all times to stop hatching young from sticking.

The incubator turns the eggs 24 times a day and we hand turn another 5 to 7 times. The eggs should be marked so that you don't keep turning them the same way. They should be turned 180 degrees one way and the same in reverse the next time. The intervals of turning should be evenly spaced. By doing this the incubators and eggs are checked regularly. Up to now we have not had time during the breeding season to weigh all the eggs. I hope to have time to do this in the coming season. Weighing eggs will indicate if they are losing enough weight during the incubation period.

Incubators should be disinfected regularly. Don't fumigate with eggs in the incubator. We move eggs into the spare incubator, then clean out the base of the empty incubator with hot water and disinfectant and, after putting together again, run it for fifteen minutes in a well-ventilated room away from the other incubators, humans and other animals. We then fumigate with potassium permanganate and formalin. Put enough potassium permanganate into a china eggcup to just cover the bottom in a little heap, and just cover the powder with the formalin. Run the incubator for a further 30 seconds, don't breathe while you are doing it. Then turn it off and run, the stuff

Fumigation. Be careful—the fumes released are dangerous

is very poisonous, so make sure the door is shut and children or livestock cannot get in. Leave the incubator for about an hour, then remove the eggcup, prop up the lid of the incubator and leave running for at least two hours. By that time the smell should have gone and the incubator be ready for use again. It is probably advisable to fumigate twice a month.

We are putting an alarm system on all our incubators this coming season. As the Centre is always manned, so far we have not had problems because the incubators are checked so often. However, I had a narrow miss last year when I found one incubator running at 104°F (40°C). Luckily I caught it in time and all the eggs hatched but it could have been a disaster. However there is no point in having an alarm system if there is no one there to listen for it. Which is another good reason for natural hatch and rear if you are leaving the house for more than two hours in any day throughout the breeding season.

Not only must the incubators and the room be kept clean, but also the handler. Wash hands and dry well before touching eggs.

Once an egg has started to pip, it is moved to the hatching incubator and placed on clean kitchen towel in a wire ring, with the pip uppermost, slightly on one side. Then we wait, and that is the hardest bit. *Falcon Propagation* suggests not touching an egg until it has pipped

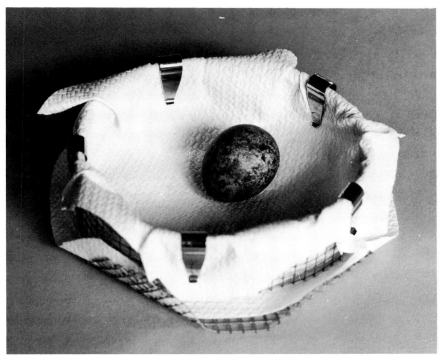

An egg in the hatching box, or ring, which is placed into the hatch

for sixty hours. If the bird is not out by then, it is possible that you may have to help. For inexperienced breeders that is a very good rule. I do occasionally intervene earlier than that if I think it is necessary, but helping eggs is difficult and injuring the hatching young is very easy. I did help out both my Egyptian Vultures and they didn't even pip. That is the first time I have done that, and luckily it turned out to be justified and both survived to adulthood. I also had to help out my first baby Secretary Bird but it sadly died within twelve hours. You have to be pretty sure that the young is going to die if you don't help, before attempting to, and that is something that only experience will tell you.

If you do try to help an egg and find that the yolk sack has not retracted, do not take the baby out, leave it in the lower half of the shell. If you can, move the egg and baby to a still-air incubator which will slow down the drying out process, fill the shell regularly with a sterile solution of water or Ringer's and do not move the

---

(*above left*) An American Screech Owl in flight (*Steven Chindgren*)
(*below left*) Two-week-old Pygmy Falcons with a four-day-old Egyptian Vulture. If there is only one baby in a clutch, put it with other youngsters that will be compatible

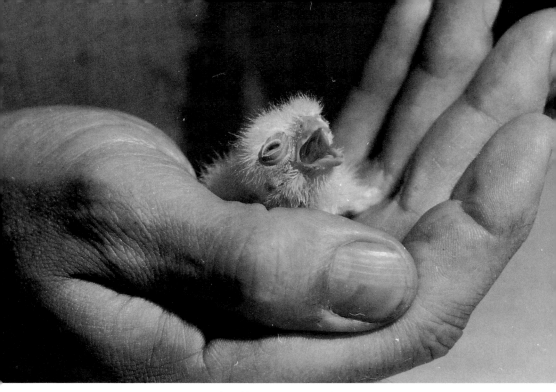

An African Pygmy Falcon baby

baby until the yolk sac has retracted. I do not consider myself an expert on incubation. I think that I am lucky and seem to have a natural feel for the eggs and young, so much so that I actually find it uncanny at times.

If you are going to go in for artificial incubation and all that it entails then you should do more homework than just reading this. The Peregrine Fund in the United States produced a booklet called *Falcon Propagation* especially for this and it is a very useful manual, the incubation side is very good. There is also *The Incubation Book* by Dr A.F. Anderson Brown. (See Bibliography.)

The main thing to remember is that you must want to be into fairly serious production of birds to work with incubation seriously. With a minimum of three incubators—and I would recommend four—candlers, weighing machines, measuring equipment, a room to put it all in, the electricity to run it all and the time to care for all of it, you are into considerable capital expenditure with no guarantee that you will get it right for several years. I would think that the contents of my incubator room and brooder room and the electricity to run them for one year must run close to £6,000. So think hard before getting too involved.

Rearing Facilities

I believe that it is a mistake to have young in the same room as eggs in incubators. Keep the two separate and then hygiene is far easier. It would not be safe, for example, to fumigate egg incubators with young birds in the same room. It's not a good idea to stay there yourself for more than about a minute. As we fumigate each incubator—seven of them—regularly, it would be very difficult to keep moving the young around to accommodate this. Baby raptors are pretty messy and droppings all over the incubators is poor maintenance. So have one place for your incubators, which can be kept clean, and one for your young.

Anyone with any sense would always have a generator available for use during power cuts. Make sure it is ready for use and have spare fuel ready for long cuts; it is sod's law that they come at night when shops and garages are closed. Eggs can stand loss of heat for longer than young, and are easier to keep warm than babies.

BROODER ROOM

It makes life much easier if the brooder room can be kept at a constant temperature. When the outside temperatures vary considerably, it is very difficult to keep young at constant temperatures, so insulate the room well. I don't intend to tell you how to do it—ask a builder or heating expert. But, having said that, don't for heaven's sake heat it with paraffin or gas and then wonder when young die from fumes. Use electricity or water radiators. Don't forget that ventilation is also important. A hot and cold water supply with a large sink should be next to the brooder room, if not in it. There is always an amazing amount of cleaning to do after each feed.

We like to have a light room for the young but don't expose them to direct sunlight as this produces the greenhouse effect and can kill them. We also have a large sign on both incubator and brooder rooms telling people to knock before entering with the death penalty for breaking the rule. It is too easy to have someone bump into you while you are handling eggs or babies, with disastrous results. With this in mind we intend putting a softer floor surface down soon so that, should a baby fall, it will not land with a crash on concrete which kills or maims. We have a work surface all round the room at a comfortable height for working. I tend to stand while working with eggs or babies, but if you prefer to sit, build the surfaces at whatever is your preferred height. Formica or some similar, easy-to-clean surface is sensible for obvious reasons.

Make sure that your feeding surface area has a 4in (10cm) lip all the way round, part of which is removable for cleaning. This should

The brooder room

prevent any baby falling should you turn your back for just a moment. The feeding area should have a non-slip surface while the birds are there. We put a piece of carpet or towel down on the feed area for the birds' comfort, so they don't slip about, moving it for cleaning. Babies will always feed better if they feel comfortable and secure.

The walls should be easy to clean as well. Tiles above the work surface for 3ft (1m) upwards are great—they can even be pretty. Don't forget that you will need a large number of power points so make sure that your wiring will stand up to it, and have a very large gin ready when you open your electricity bill.

BROODERS/INCUBATORS

The babies are usually left in the hatching incubator for about an hour, until they have dried out, unless there are a number of other hatching eggs that may be disturbed by hatched young moving around. Do not leave young in a forced air incubator for too long or they will dehydrate. When the babies are dry they are then moved to the brooder room. For babies just hatched we use two Bristol still-air incubators. These are kept at 95°F (37°C). The young are placed in containers inside the incubators and a constant check is kept on the temperature. You will need to turn on these incubators about one week before they are needed to let them settle and to make sure all is well before putting in valuable young (up goes the electricity bill again). Alarms on the brooders would be useful. Have all alarms work both ways ie for overheating as well as drops in temperature. Overheating kills eggs and babies much quicker than under-heating.

The Bristol incubators are easy to keep clean if wiped out daily, and they have good ventilation holes that we have open at all times. Rather than change the temperatures in the incubators and brooders constantly, we move the babies into cooler or hotter areas as needed. This means that we know a certain brooder should always be at a certain heat. The young stay in the incubator from four to five days. Single babies stay in longer than those with siblings or foster siblings; they need more heat with no sisters to snuggle with.

After four days or so, the young are moved from the still-air incubators into the brooders, which are water header-tanks with the bottoms removed. These are placed on the work surfaces on top of fresh newspaper which is changed at least once a day and maybe more with large numbers of young. These tanks are plastic and can be easily scrubbed out each morning; use a solution of warm water and disinfectant. Our brooders are grey; I would prefer a paler colour

Bristol incubators

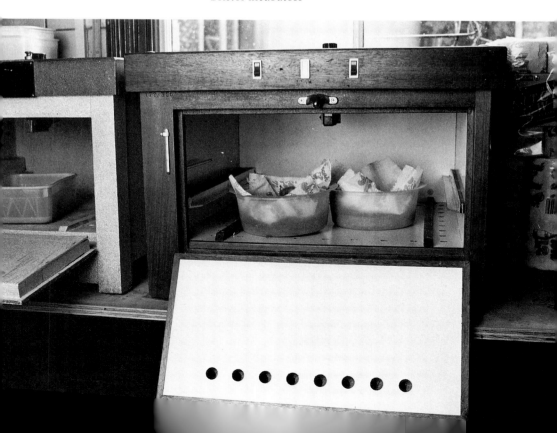

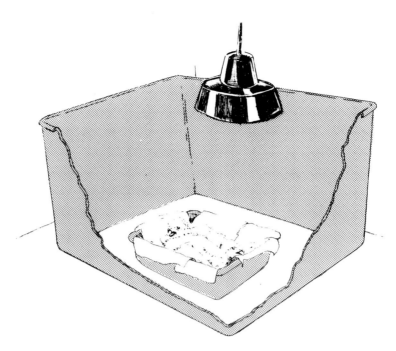

Babies in the brooder

or perhaps transparent. The heat is provided by an infra-red heat lamp suspended on a chain which can be shortened or lengthened depending on the heat required. These lamps will provide enough heat for up to twelve young over two tanks if correctly positioned. They give out no light, only heat. Always have a thermometer placed near the young to check for temperature changes. Recently I have changed our system for warming the young. Neil Forbes, our vet, got some really good heat pads which go underneath the baby containers. They only give heat when the weight of container (or adult bird when used for sick birds) is in contact with them. The heat is not that strong and they are very easy to wash. However, they are not warm enough for some young so some 'brooders' have heat from above.

The temperature in these tanks or 'brooders' varies depending on the position of the young; those nearer the lamp will be getting more heat. I have never had time to monitor the young and get enough information to be able to say that such a bird needs such a heat at a certain age. However we do have the advantage of someone always being on hand to listen for any baby that is either too hot or too cold, and believe me they will let you know in no uncertain terms.

We have the warmest brooder at about 90°F (32°C) at its centre where the heat is most direct and the other brooders each have a lower temperature. The best and (at the moment) only guide to what heat is good for what baby is, I am afraid, experience. *Falcon Propagation* says that a general rule of thumb is to reduce the temperature by 1°F each day until the young can go without heat. However, what should be remembered is that they keep their incubator and brooder rooms at an ambient temperature of between 70° to 75°F (21° to 24°C). There is absolutely no doubt that if you can afford to heat your brooder and incubator rooms to this sort of temperature life will be a lot easier and fewer problems will arise. We hope to do this for the next breeding season, at least with the brooder room.

Cold young will be very vocal while getting cold, will feel cold to the touch when cold, and will not feed well or behave in any way normally. If there are several babies together they will be huddled up, pushing one another and yelling their heads off—generally sounding pretty upset. Remember that they will usually behave in this way just after feeding as they will have lost body temperature but after ten to fifteen minutes they will settle down gently cuddled together and quiet. Hot young will also call (you will soon get to recognise the noises that mean they are upset for any reason). If in a group, they will be apart rather than together and will lie with wings and legs stretched out, sometimes panting. If they are too cold give them more heat and vice versa if they are too hot. Don't worry if you look at the young and find all of them with their heads hanging over the sides of the containers, they seem to like doing it and although it

A small container for newly hatched young

can sometimes mean they are too hot, they very often do it after all heat has been removed. The cooler you can keep the babies and still have them comfortable, the better. They seem to be much healthier and grow better if not kept too warm.

As I said early on, I have made most of the mistakes there are to make. I have, twice, left a baby in a cold weighing machine all night and it has lived, although it wasn't very happy in the morning, to say the least, but seemed to suffer no ill effects once it had warmed up. On the other hand overheating will kill babies in only one hour. So do be careful and keep a constant check. All these problems point to the sense of a well insulated, heated brooder room.

The newly hatched young going into the brooder room are placed in containers half filled with dried moss peat or sand. The Americans use a product called corn-cob litter which sounds very good. I don't think it is available in this country, nor do we seem to have a substitute. I have tried a number of other materials but always seem to come back to sand or peat, although it can be dusty. However as it is covered almost all the time, I have had no problems so far. The sand is shaped with the hand to form a deep cup. The containers we use are $1/_2$ gallon (2 litre) ice cream or margarine cartons—so get eating. They are easy to clean and can be thrown away without too much expense. They will hold a clutch of three or four Harrises, Peregrines or eagle owls for the first three or four days. Four of these containers will fit into our still-air incubators and the brooders. You can get seven young Pygmy Falcons into them for ages.

The sand is covered with two pieces of kitchen towel which is replaced after every feed, ie four times a day except for tiny young such as the Pygmy Falcons who are fed more often. This keeps the young fairly clean and means that you can check on the droppings regularly. Reshape the cup with your fist each time you clean out the babies, flat or slippery surfaces are very dangerous and cause splayed legs in less than half an hour. Make sure the peat or sand is dry and have further dry supplies ready for when it is needed. We buy those huge bags of Irish moss peat from garden centres. The peat is usually pretty wet when you buy it, so the bags have to be opened and dried well some time before the peat will be required.

Once the young have got too big to be able to move about in these containers, larger ones will be needed. We use washing up bowls, half filled with sand or peat and with kitchen towel on top as usual. Again, make sure that the surface is not too flat. We did have some problems with young Snowy Owls. Snowy Owls and other large eagle owls get pretty heavy before they start to stand. When the young had disturbed the kitchen towel, and were sitting on just the sand, they drove the particles of sand into their joints, so I prefer to use peat for the larger owls. It doesn't seem to matter if the young

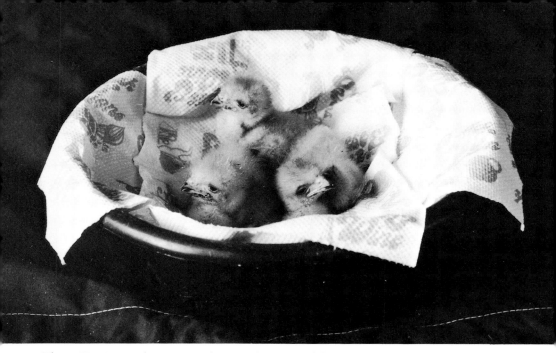

Three Harris Hawks in a washing-up bowl—half-filled with peat and covered with tissues

swallow small amounts of peat if they drop food on it. It comes up again as a brown casting.

If I have young that tend to climb out of the bowls, or Tawny Eagles who are busy leaping all barriers so that they can beat one another up, I use a cardboard box with higher sides, with peat and kitchen towel. We just throw it away after two or three days. Use old ones from your local shop—it is good conservation, but make sure they didn't have washing powder in before as that is bad for the birds.

The young remain in the brooder room until the DoE rings will stay on. This will be ten to fourteen days depending on the sex and the species—older with eagles. If you have to put on double rings for sensitive species, place the larger ring on first, then the small ring. This will hold on the larger ring, meaning that you can return the baby at an earlier stage. The small ring will need to be removed at about four weeks if the baby turns out to be female. You need not bother to remove the larger one, if the baby is male, until removing the young from the parents when they are hard down.

Once the rings stay on, the young are returned to the parents or foster parents, to make room for the next batch.

Food and Supplements

In the last three years The Falconry Centre has done some work on different food types with the assistance of a zoology student from Swansea University—with some interesting results. Having been fairly convinced that day-old cockerels were a poor food source, I am now of the opinion that for some species they are better than a higher protein food such as quail. Having said that, I am also convinced that no *one* food source is good for either young or adult birds.

FOOD TYPES

The Centre uses a variety of foods. The main diet for most of the young is DOC, with mice, rats, quail and grown-on chicks to add variety. For the *accipiters*, like European Sparrowhawks, Black Sparrowhawks and Goshawks, we use a higher protein diet, probably quail. I have found that Black Sparrowhawks are very fussy, and if started on quail, will refuse mice and rats which have a strong taste (they smell vile when being minced as well, especially the mice). So we try to mix foods with birds that may get wedded to one particular type. The owl species that we have reared have done pretty well on DOC, with mouse and rat. The buzzards such as Common, Redtailed and Ferruginous have also done well on a similar diet to the owls, although we did have problems with Redshouldered Buzzards. But that was many years ago and I think we could probably do better now.

We found, however, that a diet of pure quail was not good for *buteos* and owls and could kill them. It seemed to be too high-protein and gave them diarrhoea, occasionally so badly that they died. We do not use quail on these species. Eagles and Harris Hawks can grow well on almost anything, so we feed a mixed diet of all food types. I do occasionally add a little good beef for the bigger birds. Falcons can also do well on any of the food types and we have reared them on pure diets of DOC, rats, mice and quail. Blyth's Hawk Eagles were interesting and at first quite terrifying, as they ate about a quarter the weight of food that a similar size bird would eat and grew very slowly, but did well on a mixed diet.

SUPPLEMENTS

We add supplements to the diets of all the species; Vydex do a really good range of supplements and have good written information on them as well. Add a pinch to the food once every two days. If you overdo it, you can kill the young. We had one gentleman phone us up during the breeding season, worried sick because his young Harrises were dying. Now it is quite difficult to diagnose over the phone, and after asking him all the usual questions and he seemed to be doing everything right, just by chance we asked him how much supplement he was putting on and were told that there was a teaspoonful put on four times a day; hey presto—dead babies.

Be very careful with calcium additives. It is too easy to cause an imbalance. We lost a number of young owls years ago when feeding sterilised bone flour, which was then giving an imbalance of phosphate and causing the babies' bodies to think they were short of calcium, thus causing dreadful rickets. We use no calcium at all. If you feel that you should, then use calcium lactate or calcium carbonate.

PREPARATION
All our quail, mice and rats are frozen before they get to us. The DOCs are sometimes fresh, but nowadays come from our frozen stock. So once food has been thawed and prepared for feeding to babies it cannot be frozen again safely. This means that food *must* be prepared daily. We have found with large numbers of young, that mincing is the quickest way to prepare food. All DOC are skinned (I must have skinned millions over the years) and then minced. We have murdered several Kenwood mincers which are really not designed to mince chicken or quail, and as for rats—they just finish the motors completely. So, nowadays, as my husband was a great believer in the right tool for the job, we have a Hobart commercial mincer which will mince whole rats without batting an eyelid. If you are clever, and have a good machine, when mincing DOC you will find that all the meat arrives first through the mincer and then all the yolk. As you do not want most of that yolk you can switch containers and end up with one full of good food that is not too wet and one full of what looks like a good spaghetti bolognese sauce. Throw the sauce away and use the good gear.

Rats and mice we mince whole and as we feed using forceps (tweezers) any really furry bits we discard. Quail we skin and cut off the feet and wings, gut and mince the rest. As quail, rat and mouse are somewhat dry we have a dish of warm water ready when feeding and dip each forceful in the water before offering to the baby. The prepared food is kept in very clean tupperware type containers in the fridge (not to be mistaken with the pâté!). The food should be warmed for the babies but to keep warming and then cooling any remains is not good, so we feed straight from the fridge or warm the right amount first.

Feeding Young Birds

As a general rule, don't feed any newly hatched young. We wait about seven hours after hatching before giving the first feed. Pygmy Falcons we will feed earlier. But apart from very small babies such as Pygmy Falcons who weigh about 5g at hatching and need extra feeds, we feed all our young four times a day. We may add one extra feed for the first couple of days with small birds, European Sparrowhawks and American Kestrels for example.

Firstly the food is prepared for the day. There is nothing worse than running out of food halfway through the last feed, and having to prepare more, when you are really dying to go to bed. We weigh our babies before and after every feed and although this is not necessary, there is no doubt that it saves lives. As soon as you have a problem with a baby it will stop gaining weight, and if this can be spotted immediately action can be taken. So after preparing the food, the babies are weighed and their weights marked down on each bird's individual chart. Then they are fed. The babies can either be fed while in their containers on the feed surface, or moved out onto a non-slip surface on the feed area and fed there. We do both. The food container should be close to you with the already mentioned bowl of water to dampen the food. I find a curved pair of forceps is the easiest way of feeding young. Some people use a plastic bag with a hole and squeeze the food into the bird's mouth. To use your fingers is slow and hard work. We round off the ends of the forceps. I have had people say that they are worried about the babies' eyes; all I can say is that I have never had a problem and will continue to use forceps until I can find something that I consider works better.

Some young do better if fed in the hand when they are tiny. If they are not feeding when in the hand you are probably not holding them so that they feel secure. Most people don't hold them correctly to start with. It is just a matter of trial and error to get it right.

Each baby is given as much as it will eat, except for Sakers and

Feeding three young Pygmy Falcons. Note the carpet they are sitting on, which prevents slipping. It is difficult to keep tiny babies clean

Peregrines who are so greedy they will go on feeding until the food comes so far up their throats it falls out again. The thing to remember is that *if* a baby has any food still in its crop at the next feed then don't feed it, or at least only give it a very small amount. So always check the crop before feeding and gently turn the baby over and look at its stomach, if it is very hard then don't feed the baby. Feeling the bird's stomach is the only way to tell if an owl has digested its last meal. Although we have never heard of anyone killing babies by underfeeding, many people have killed them by overfeeding.

After they are all fed we re-weigh all the babies, chart their fed weight, then they are put back into clean containers with fresh kitchen towel. The brooders are scrubbed, all surfaces wiped and fresh newspaper put down, forceps are washed and kept in a solution of Milton. Peace reigns in the brooder room and the brooder technician can now go and get dressed and have breakfast.

And so it goes on. We only scrub brooders once a day, but the young are cleaned out after each feed. The feeds are normally at 8am (food preparation 7.00–7.30am start depending on amount of food to be prepared), 12.30pm, 6.00pm, 11pm or later. These times are just what suits us here. Often they are not kept to if other problems arise and have to be attended to, but generally we try to keep a routine for the babies as they do better on it.

In my opinion owls are probably the most difficult to rear and I think it is because they have no crop and so it is easier to overfeed them. They are far more likely to get diarrhoea than other species. So be careful not to overfeed any of the owls. We have found that many of the owl species open their eyes on day one and close them again immediately. All the owls need to have the sides of their beaks touched with the food for them to respond and feed. We also make ourselves sound like complete idiots by hooting to all the *strix* family, although I am damned if I am going to attempt the piglike grunting that adult Snowy Owls produce. Silly though it may sound, many of the young respond to vocalisation. We chup away to falcons and make a very weird selection of noises to various other species all with great effect, if only to have visitors sniggering as they listen to us.

Falcons lift up their heads and like to have the food placed into their beaks preferably touching the roof of their mouths which seems to make them swallow. All the buzzards, hawks, kites and eagles like to see the food coming at just above eye height and they will snatch at it at the last moment. Baby vultures are the same. There will always be the odd difficult baby. Leave him (undoubtedly) until last and concentrate on him alone; then he may do better. I have had some real pigs to cope with. The first Black Sparrowhawk, male of course, was very nearly strangled many times on late-night feeds. It would take an hour to feed all the other babies and another hour to feed him.

IDENT.	PARENTS. H.H.2.	SPECIES. HARRIS HAWK	HATCH DATE 11ᵗ JUNE	TIME. very early AM.	W.T. MKD.

DAY	DATE	WT.F1.	WT.F2	WT.F3.	WT.F4	COMMENTS.
1	11/6/86	39.6 41.5	40.5 42.5	41.5 44.2		
2	12/6	40.9 43.9	43 47.2	43 49.6	68.3 52	
3	13/6	48 51.9	48.2 50	48.5 52.3	49.3 55.8	
4	14/6	50.1 54.8	52.3 58.3	55.5 61.3	58.7 64.7	
5	15/6	57.4 63.9	61.3 66.1	63 71.5	69.7 77.2	
6	16/6	68.7 76.9	75.4 86.6	83.9 93.6	90.5 96.2	
7	17/6	86.7 97.4	94 105.2	99.2 105.1	100.6 108.5	
8	18/6	106.1 112	108.9 122.2	117.6 127.5	123.1 132.6	
9	19/6	123 132.7	129 145	139.8 153.2	—	not hungry.
10	20/6	139.3 151.3	— 158.6	172.1 166	180	not weighed - forgot!
11	21/6	164.3 176.5	173.8 191.9	184 202.8	193.8 212	
12	22	193.8 208.5				
13	23/6	224.6				w. once per day.
14	24/6	253.7				Back to parents.

IDENT.	PARENTS. MR & MRS TIMMS	SPECIES. TAWNY EAGLE	HATCH DATE 1/2/84	TIME. Early AM.	W.T. MKD.

DAY	DATE	WT.F1.	WT.F2	WT.F3.	WT.F4	COMMENTS.
1	1/2/84			51.5	52.75	
2	2/2	51.6 53.6	53 55.5	55.2 58.1	56.9 61.3	
3	3/2	59.6 64.7	62.3 69.8	68.4 74.3	— —	last feed - still had crop.
4	4/2	65.9 72.0	69.2 76.2	73.3 77.8	74 82.2	
5	5/2	76.6 85.7	82.7 88.9	85.7 95	91.3 98	
6	6/2	89.8 99.7	97.6 100	98 105.3	102.6 109	
7	7/2	101.5 110	106.2 116.9	111.5 123.6	116.8 124.2	
8	8/2	117.0 134.4	127.8 138.8	133.1 147.8	142.1 147.2	
9	9/2	137 148	— —	141.3 154.8	148 161.1	not hungry at lunch time.
10	10/2	152.1 159.8	167 180.2	176.2 189.5	185 196.1	
11	11/2	187 208.5	206.6 228.9	221 244.1	235.5 251	
12	12/2	232 266.2				teaching to feed itself
13	13/2	2)5				
14	14/2	380				

IDENT. 0198 W. 1115 V.	PARENTS. PEPPER & CHUCKS	SPECIES. PEREGRINE (P. minor).	HATCH DATE MAY 8ᵗ (?)	TIME. 11.45 pm.	W.T. MKD.

DAY	DATE	WT.F1	WT.F2.	WT.F3.	WT.F4	COMMENTS.
1	8/5/85	30.1 31.7	30.8 32.9	32.2 34.2		
2	9/5	32.6 36.2	34.9 38	36.5 39.6	37 41.1	
3	10/5	39.1 43.7	41.9 45.5	43.5 48.7	47.9 50.5	
4	11/5	46.2 50.0	48.1 52.5	51.5 54.9	52.7 56.8	
5	12/5	53.4 59.3	56.4 4.9	59.6 65.2	63.1 72.1	
6	13/5	67.3 74.3	73 80	76.5 89	84.6 90.5	
7	14/5	80.6				Doing well. onto once per day.
8	15/5	96.4				
9	16/5	116				
10	17/5	138				
11	18/5	153				
12	19/6	176				
13	24/5	201				
	BACK TO PARENTS (HOORAY).					

Feed charts

Baby Great Horned Owls

Don't panic if young birds of prey won't eat, and miss a feed, think how often in the wild they have to survive a pretty lean time. If you are sensible and think about what you are doing, rearing is pretty easy.

Returning Young

We have tried several methods of returning young and very occasionally we have had accidents. But as far as I can remember we have only had three birds die, two of which were Goshawks who were too old when replaced and bailed out of the nest. They were not hurt by the parents but died of exposure. One young Peregrine which I put back too early was too young to go in with older siblings. All three deaths could have been avoided had I been more careful.

We have had to remove young from parents who were obviously going to harm them and we have had parents who just refuse to feed the young. But generally they will take them back if you have courage. The pleasure of seeing them cover those babies and feed them is just wonderful.

If we have bred a species we have never bred before and want to return the young to the parent birds, we put back a youngster of a different species that is less important but of the same or similar family group. We watch the response of the parents and then later exchange the foster baby for the real one. We do have a great advantage in that we have many birds and so always have the chance of foster parents or foster babies being available.

When returning young, the egg or eggs are removed carefully and the young placed back in the nest. Food is also put on the nest ledge for the parents. The lucky person getting the job may then stay in the pen, well away from the nest, just for the first few minutes in case there is immediate aggressive action. Otherwise he or she will come out, leaving the door on the latch, but not locked, for quick access if needed. Nine times out of ten, nothing happens for ages. One of us will sit and watch the birds for several hours. We will try to choose a warmish dry day so that the baby does not get cold, and will put the bird in without a feed so that it may call when hungry. If the weather is good and there are several babies they can do without being covered at least during daylight, and on warm nights through the night as well. Falcons are the easiest to put back as they are very greedy and will call readily for food and they seem fearless. Young owls are pretty good too but all the rest tend to collapse in a heap if the parent bird comes near and they are unlikely to feed the first day back.

Signs of aggression are fairly obvious. If one of the parents picks up a baby, move fast and bang loudly on the side of the pen while you get in there, the noise usually stops them. Some adults may bite at the young or even foot them occasionally, but you will see if it is just to get a reaction or is serious. Sometimes a parent will cover young immediately and then we breathe a sigh of relief and leave them alone, just going back to check them regularly. Sometimes one or other parent will keep flying over to look at the baby showing no signs of aggression but obviously worried by the rapid growth of their eggs. We are usually hopeful if this happens.

This point in the breeding cycle is where your aviary design will be very useful to you if you have got it right. You need to be able to see the nest ledge easily without disturbing the parents. If the young are covered, you just have to watch for them being fed. You may not see the actual feeding but if they went in with empty crops and then have full ones, things are going okay. Don't panic if they are not fed for 36 hours. They can survive that time easily at 14 days old. I think it would be true to say that if the parents are not going to take the young back you will usually know within 3 or 4 hours. If the young are not covered by dark and the weather is bad, they will have to be removed after dark and returned again the following morning. Feed them that night but not in the morning before they are returned. It is when there are no signs that it is difficult to decide what to do.

The advantage of putting in two-week-old young is that they are normally large enough to be grabbed once and still survive. We have only had one bird permanently injured since we started returning young in 1977, nevertheless it is pretty nerve-wracking the first few times. But you will get the idea of when the bird is just curious and when it seriously want to injure the young. I am afraid that it is not a clear-cut process nor something that I can describe in words; it is very often a gut feeling and you just seem to know if things are going right or wrong.

Once a pair has accepted young and reared them you are in the happy position of knowing their capabilities and using them to your full advantage. Some of our pairs are wonderful. Our old female Saker will watch us come in with the young while she is still sitting on the the second clutch of eggs and, if we put the young on the opposite end of the nest ledge, she just gets up, leaving the eggs and walks over to the young tucking them under her while gently pushing one's hand away from the ledge.

FOSTER PARENTS

At The NBoP Centre we have had great success in fostering our young. We have found that as long as we stick to the same family group or a very close one, there are no problems with parents and young giving the wrong feeding signals. We put falcons with falcons and have had all sorts of species rearing foster children—Peregrines rearing Lanners, Sakers rearing Peregrines, Lanners and Sakers all at one time. Barbary Falcons rearing Merlins and even American Kestrels. Prairies rearing African Peregrines and so on. We have mixed up Harrises, Redtails, Ferruginous and Common Buzzards with various parents of all those species and even had a Redtail rearing a Tawny Eagle along with her own young.

Many of my owls will rear other species of owls and often, by the end of the season, I can never remember who is with whom. We also give parent birds a larger number than they might normally have as we can supply enough food for them to manage. This is why it is a good idea to have a fairly large nest ledge because you must remember the amount of room five young Goshawks take up prior to them being able to fly.

As we are so keen to have our young parent-reared, we may keep a couple of pairs of birds that are not perhaps earning their keep by producing young but who are worth their weight in gold as rearing birds.

Once the parents have accepted the young, an eye must still be kept on the eyasses. The nest floor must not get too flat or leg problems may occur. Plenty of good quality food must be made available at all times, but not just piled in in the morning and left to go off. The young must be ringed at ten to fourteen days, depending on the sex and species. One idea with young that hatch over an extended period is to put a little Elastoplast over the ring if you think it will slip off. This should hold it in place until the leg is grown enough

Various baby Eagle Owls

to keep the ring on, and means the birds only have to be disturbed once instead of several times.

Young must be watched once they start to leave the nest. If the pen is not totally roofed over, young that are out of the nest, especially if they are on the floor of the pen, must be moved under cover or back to the nest ledge when it is close to dark in wet or very cold weather.

Young Goshawks are in our experience the most difficult to put back. Most young birds are frightened of the natural parents to start with, although falcons tend to be so relaxed and greedy they don't seem to bother much. But the hawks cower at the sight of these frightening adults in the beginning. If young Gosses are left too late, and are getting mobile, which they do very early, they will try to get off the nest ledge to get away from the parents or foster parents. So young Gosses should always be put back as early as possible to avoid this problem.

Don't remove successfully reared young until they are hard down and flying. If you move them before they are hard down, fret marks may well appear on the feathers. The only time I like to remove young early is if they are going straight into a new breeding pen and not going to be flown, in which case I like them to settle into the new pen before they fly really well. This usually means that they will not crash around once they are flying, as they have already got used to their new home.

Aviary Space

As I am sure you all know, building pens is very expensive and time consuming. However to produce reasonable numbers of quality birds, space, over and above the space for the breeding pairs, will be needed. Some very good parents do not mind just-fledged young being removed and fourteen-day-old babies replacing them; this is very valuable for those people short on adult rearing birds. However the elder young have then got to go somewhere to finish growing. We have found that with birds such as Harris Hawks it is a very good idea to remove them from the parents as soon as they are hard down and put them into a spacious pen where they can fly around, forget their parents and become independent before being taken out and trained. The reason for this is that Harrises may tend to get noisy if removed from parents immediately they are hard down and then cut down to be trained. If left for a month to get away from being fed by parents and instantly having the parent replaced by a human, they will be all the better for it.

Our aim is to produce good birds and we have found that the extra expense of spare pens for the young is well worth it. The

Black Sparrowhawk on a bow perch

pens can always be used for other birds during the early spring and winter months.

Problems

If the brooder room is built carefully, the incubators and brooders well maintained and hygiene is of a good standard, there should be few problems with hand rearing. However there is always the chance of babies getting infection. Very often these infections tend to be some sort of enteritis, although not always. This is where the weighing machine comes into its own as weight will not only spot a problem baby, but will inform of its progress. Any sick baby should be taken away from the others and put in a brooder on its own. Mute samples should be taken immediately to the nearest Poultry Laboratory, and if we think it may be something more serious than an upset tummy we may well use a broad spectrum antibiotic.

One or two things have to be remembered when using an antibiotic without knowing it is the right one. It may not be the right drug for the infection. It could kill bacteria that *should* be there. Babies will get dehydrated on many drugs so give plenty of liquids. If a baby goes off its feed then it can be kept going on liquids while the problem is being sorted out. For runny tummies we use a super powder called Forgastrin, sprinkled on the food, it works wonders very quickly. But don't make the mistake of immediately stuffing the baby with food when it starts to recover. Biosol and IonAid are also useful preparations for babies that are off their feed, and will keep them going for some time.

Call the vet if you have problems, and if you feel that he or she is not experienced in coping with baby raptors then ask him or her to phone one of the vets known to be experienced, for advice. As already mentioned, if they will not do this then change your vet. But don't leave calling him until the baby is at death's door or he won't have a hope in hell of being able to help you and that is not fair on the vet. Keep the sick baby warm, and give plenty of fluids and do all you can to find out the problem, but don't overhandle it—imagine how you would feel with some giant mauling you every ten minutes.

It is a good idea to have a cupboard with one or two standby drugs on hand for problems, also 1ml insulin syringes which are perfect if babies need to be injected. With weak babies I may inject a solution called Duphalyte just to help them get going.

Only those people who have struggled for days with a sick baby can understand the strain which is put on the person rearing. After a prolonged time handling a sick baby that continues downhill, one tends to be relieved if it finally dies. However, don't let sick babies get you down. There will always be the baby that should not survive, just as there is in the wild.

Since starting to write this epic, one or two other problems have arisen. If by any chance you hatch birds that are physically wrong, such as the blind Ferruginous that I now have produced, put them down. It is wrong to risk them breeding in the hands of people who may be more interested in money than the future offspring from deformed or incorrect birds. It is a hard thing to do, especially when a lot of effort has been put into producing that young, but it is the only moral thing to do. The adult pair should then be either split up, or not allowed to breed again.

Disposal of Surplus Birds

Having spent all that time and effort producing good birds, I actually hate to see them go. On the other hand, when people who have had birds from The Falconry Centre contact us and tell us how pleased they are with them, or what they have caught with them, we are really pleased.

Recently, to try to ensure that all our birds go to knowledgeable homes, we have asked all potential new owners to send us a letter giving us more information. I like to know what bird they want (you would be surprised at the number of people who don't know), why they want it, what experience they have, what sort of quarry they are going to fly at and what sort of countryside they are going to fly the bird over. All these questions are relevant and will tell you a great deal about the prospective owner. We also ask for a photo of the quarters they have for the birds. Occasionally someone refuses to comply with these questions and requests and gets difficult, but when we point out that this process is in the interest of the birds and the reputation of breeders and falconry, most people are very helpful. Some of the quarters in the photos are far nicer than my house. If we are not happy we will suggest alterations to the quarters for the birds and if these are done then all is well. One gentleman did try to get birds by using photos of someone else's quarters but we caught him out and the gentleman in question left the premises without the birds. I cannot put down what he said.

Breeders should be prepared to let young be vetted by the vet of the prospective new owner, just as would happen if you were buying a horse, if you were sensible. The fee will have to be paid by the new owner and appointment times convenient to both parties should be made.

It takes a little effort on both sides to do all this but it has to be good for all of us in the long run and, what is more important, good for the birds. This is after all what we should all be aiming for if we are producing a living creature.

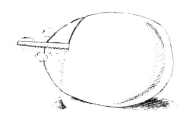

6 PREVENTIVE MEDICINE

To quote Neil Forbes in one of his published papers: 'All birds, both parents and offspring are in a constant balance between health and disease.' As captive birds are the responsibility of the keeper, it is up to all of us to keep that balance correct. The best way to cope with any illness or injuries in captive birds of prey is to try and avoid them in the first place. Although this may sound rather trite, it is amazing how many problems can be solved by better care of birds, or spotting possible problems very early and treating immediately.

As stated so often throughout this book, get a good interested vet close by sorted out before you get a bird, or if not then, at least before you get any problems. (I shall use 'him' when speaking of vets just to shorten things, fully realising that there are just as many female vets, including my own cousin, all of whom are as expert with birds of prey.)

We have three first-class vets fairly close to The NBoP Centre and they all take calls from and give advice to other less experienced vets who have the sense to call them. It is so much better to have your local vet, while he has you and the bird with him, call an expert to discuss the problem, rather than take the bird miles for more expert advice. The more this is done, the more your own vet will learn, and the more experienced vets we will have generally. If you or your local vet feel that an examination by someone more experienced will be of benefit, you may have to travel with the bird. Incidentally, I had a phone call the other day from a falconer who had problems with his bird. He horrified me somewhat by saying that he could not afford to take his bird to the vet for treatment. If you cannot afford to care for a bird properly, and that includes veterinary treatment, then without doubt you should not have a bird in the first place.

Because of the Zoo Licensing Act 1981, we have to have a regular vet inspection here. Our vet comes round the Centre every eight weeks. This is very helpful, as his fresh, experienced eye may spot something that we, seeing the birds every day, may not have noticed. Although I don't think everyone need do this, it is certainly a good idea for those people with numbers of birds in pens for breeding.

Annual Clean and Check

At least once a year, preferably more often, every bird is checked over, those in pens being caught up. This gives time for pens to be cleaned and checked over at the same time. The birds can be put into either temporary holding pens or boxes. We tend to clean pens and check birds by blocks. Each pair of birds in a particular breeding block, or half a block, is caught up and boxed separately. The pen is then cleaned. If you have large numbers of pens, why not organise a pen-cleaning weekend with friends who are willing to help. Then when they want to clean their pens you can return the favour. This will get the work done quickly.

Don't forget to have all necessary materials ready before starting as they may be difficult to get, particularly at a weekend. If you have any vegetation on the floor of the pen, clear all this first and remove from the pen. Check all walls, wire or netting for any faults (which, if found, should be repaired immediately), scrub down with a strong solution of disinfectant, rinsing with clean water afterwards. Empty nest ledges and scrub and rinse in the same way. Check over all perches for rough or sharp bits, replace any worn ones, scrub and rinse. The same goes for food ledges and baths.

If you do not have gravel on the floor, but just soil, it will by this time be mud because of all the water, and you will wish you did have gravel. Give it a thorough raking, removing all faeces and rubbish, then sprinkle with the weed killer Prefix, which will stop growth for about a year. Cover the Prefix with a good spread of sand, dry if possible, this will stop the birds touching the weed killer and will dry the pen out. If you do have gravel as a base, first shovel out any really heavily soiled areas. Wash it down, with a high pressure hose if you can borrow or hire one. Most of these have a facility which enables you to add disinfectant to the water. Rinse well and add more gravel if needed. Leave the pen for as long as possible giving it time to dry out a little (twelve hours) before returning the birds.

Birds from pens which are finished at the end of the day can stay in their boxes overnight, to give the pen time to dry out. If the boxes are placed somewhere dark, quiet, dry and not too hot or cold, it does the birds no harm, particularly if you have good boxes. I reiterate the need for good equipment and my constant surprise at the poor boxes people use in which to place valuable birds. It really is neither difficult nor expensive to have a store of good, clean, strong wooden boxes for holding birds. They can even be built to fit inside one another for storage. Clean carpet on the floor of a *good* light-proof box will keep a bird perfectly safe and quiet for twenty-four hours, particularly a well fed aviary bird. I have travelled two-week-old eyass raptors all the way from southern Africa to this country and they have been in the boxes for twenty-four hours with no problems at all. Do not put more than one bird per box, even with known compatible pairs. Birds of prey should always be boxed individually unless they are small babies.

Once you are ready to put the birds back, then is the time to check them over, *not* before. If you can have a vet there at that time, that is even better management. Have a typed standby check list that you use every time.

External Check
- Weight or bodily condition
- Feathers—look for parasites and feather damage. Parasites can be found by wrapping a piece of sticking plaster the wrong way round your finger and running it through the feathers.
- Eyes—clear and healthy, with no filming over.
- Wings—watch the joints.
- Feet—look for redness and heat or swelling.
- Mutes—look for staining of vent.
- Oral check—the inside of the mouth should be nice and pink.
- Nasal cavities—check clear.
- Check the rings for clarity and comfortable fit.

Internal Check
- Check respiration and heart rates, listen for noises.
- Take a mute sample and have it tested.

It is a good idea to spray for parasites and worm the birds anyway, to avoid having to recatch should any be present in the mute samples.

Harris Hawk

For external parasites, we use either Johnson's Antimite or Alugan spray, not the powder. Always spray the bird out of doors, never inside or in a confined space. Hold the spray well away from the bird and watch you don't spray eyes, its or yours. Make sure the under wings and tail are sprayed, and the back of the head (see also page 200).

For internal parasites, such as worms, we use Panacur wormer for dogs and cattle. We give this orally with a plastic 1ml syringe for most birds, using a larger syringe and a tube for the eagles and vultures. The dosage is 1ml per 1kg body-weight (Neil Forbes). This wormer is better than the sheep wormer of the same name as it has higher strength and less has to be given. It can also be obtained in small quantities, the sheep wormer gives you enough for a whole flock of sheep.

For catching birds the quickest and best way is to use a landing net. Few birds apart from the really large eagles, won't fit a good−sized one. The advantage of the net is that the bird grabs at the mesh with its talons, keeping the foot open, and rarely punctures its own feet, which is very likely to happen if you catch a bird by hand. When catching up any bird of prey for whatever reason, cut the sharp tips off all the talons. The only exception to this is birds that are just about to be released to the wild and which need sharp talons for survival. If you leave the bird in the net while trimming the talons, there is even less likelihood of it wounding itself. Use a good small pair of electrical wire-cutters, but don't cut too much off or the talon will bleed copiously. This is bound to happen occasionally; we usually hold the bird until the bleeding stops, put on antibiotic powder and, if we have cut much too high, an ordinary fabric Elastoplast to keep the wound clean for a couple of days. The plaster will come off of its own accord. Then if catching the bird for pen cleaning, put it into the box and don't do the rest of the examination and worming until just before releasing back to the pen.

If a bird has cut its own foot with a talon, clean the place well, dress with antibiotic powder or cream, cover with a plaster and leave. Birds' cuts seem to heal much better if the birds are put

Wallberg's Eagle

back into pens and can move around, keeping their circulation good, rather than confined in small compartments where their circulation will not be half so active.

Beaks should be checked for excessive growth, top and bottom mandibles. It is often difficult to spot overgrowth in lower mandibles when birds are loose in pens, but easy when examining by hand. The lower mandible will sometimes be too long, but more often the two sides will start to curl inwards, trapping food and sometimes leading to discomfort or infection. This excessive growth of beak can be easily nibbled back with the cutters. The upper mandible may be too long, in which case cut it back with the wire-cutters. It is possible to cut it back too far, cutting into the quick and causing it to bleed. Again, clean the cut, but don't dress. Make sure that the bird is given very well slashed food for about a week, so that the discomfort of a sore beak does not stop it feeding.

I have heard that some people take blood samples from birds of prey by cutting the beak back to the quick and catching the blood. Personally I think this is potty, and poor management. Our blood samples are taken from the bird's wing, and *always* by a good vet. Not only is this safer for the bird, but it gives you an independent witness for the sample taking, which could be useful if you ever needed it in a court case.

The tooth on the beak of falcons can cause problems, particularly in small falcons such as Merlins. It will sometimes split, and if not caught early the split can go right up to the cere, causing enormous problems. Food gets lodged in the split, further widening it and risking infection. The bird should have the split cut from the side with cutters. Usually the beak will flake away to the end of the split. Great care must be taken. We then file the beak down until the split has gone, using small engineering files. You may end up with a bird that looks a little odd, but it must be done. The beak should be evened up on both sides so that pressure is not put too much on one point. If the split is very bad, take the bird to someone who knows what they are doing, if you are worried about tackling it yourself. Car-body filler can be used to fill cracks that are difficult to file back but again, advice should be taken.

When physically casting (holding a bird bodily), it is much easier, and better for the bird's plumage, to wrap it in a teacloth or lightweight towel. This means the bird is firmly held and the primaries cannot crack if it struggles. I am very unhappy about birds being held on their backs. I much prefer them held upright when in the hand and on their fronts on tables. There will be times when it is unavoidable, but if it is avoidable then I would always recommend *not* holding them on their backs. I have seen them die that way. Birds with any heart or respiratory problems should never be held thus. A cushion put on a table before placing the bird there will give the bird something, other than its own feet, to hold on to.

I read in one paper of a vet suggesting that most birds of prey will lie still on their backs while being weighed, or examined, if the examiner moves slowly. My only answer is that if that approach was tried on most of my birds he or she would very soon change his mind. It is always better to have at least two people for examining birds, one to hold and one to examine. With big birds, particularly when taking blood samples, we have three people.

Foot Problems

Feet in birds of prey tend to have poor circulation. If there are any small cuts or punctures, infection can and does get in. Bumblefoot, as it is generally called, can be very difficult to cure unless caught in the early stages. Without doubt, 99 per cent of bumblefoot is caused by poor perching, both for tethered birds and birds in pens. It is vital to get perching right, both for the mental and physical comfort of the bird. It was interesting to note that when we built the Eagle Barn this year, two pairs of relatively tame vultures were in pens in the barn over the somewhat extended five month finishing period. Because they were tame we could work in pens around them finishing the work, moving the vultures anytime we wanted to work on the pen they inhabited. Consequently the birds had slightly differently placed perches each time they were moved. It was easy to notice that they were very much happier in some pens than in others, although the inside of each pen was absolutely identical apart from perch positions. Once we had established which perches they were happiest with we altered those in the pens they were to have as their final home and, hurrah, happy, comfortable birds.

The physical comfort is easier to get right and even more important in the prevention of foot problems. Make sure that the timber used for perches is not too hard (very old seasoned timber gets like iron) and there are no rough or sharp edges. Give the option of a rounded piece of timber on the edge of the nest ledge. A rock or rounded concrete lump in the pen will often be used and keeps talons down. The edge of the bath should be wide and rounded. No squared timber should be used unless the edges have been planed off. You should be able to run your hand along all possible perching areas and not get any splinters.

The Peregrine Fund use a platform perch in each pen with a coconut doormat on top. The perch is slightly angled down so that it does not hold moisture and many of the birds love it. I like the idea but haven't used it in the Eagle Barn as the platform would have to be enormous. However, with falcons—which is basically all the Peregrine Fund and the World Center for Birds of Prey at Boise, Idaho, deal with—it is a good idea. Falcons tend to be more susceptible to bumblefoot than other species, apart from Sparrowhawks.

With birds that are tethered, it is a good idea to give a choice of two perches. Two perches for the birds to choose from will make their life more interesting and keep their feet in better condition. We use 1 to 2in (2.5 to 5cm) thick cork on the top of our blocks. It is easy to clean and disinfect, and does not get too cold in freezing weather. With birds that may have had foot problems, we give a softer padded block. I like padded bow perches as well, particularly with any of the sparrowhawk family. Both European Sparrowhawks and Black Sparrowhawks have fine delicate skin and this can easily get worn and sore on a hard perch.

At the first sign of heat, redness or swelling get the bird to a vet. A good vet should take a swab of the infection before prescribing any drugs as the infection can take several forms, some of which are susceptible to certain drugs and some to others. If the infection is not responding within a week, go back to the vet and ask to try another drug, or surgery may be required. When treating birds, for heaven's sake remember to give the full course of drugs if they have been prescribed. Giving only half a course and stopping because the infection seems to clear up can be fatal. The infection may come back and be harder to control the next time. So if a five-day course is prescribed, go the full five days, not four.

Not all lumps and bumps on feet are likely to be bumblefoot. There will be the occasional corn, again, these are usually caused by poor perches. Hunting birds will sometimes get a thorn in a foot or leg. This will often show as a lump later on, with no heat or reddening. These can often be squeezed and the lump will pop out. Dress and cover the hole to stop infection getting in and it should heal with no problems. However, whatever the problem, it is always best to get a vet to look at it early on, rather than wait and have an infection grow worse. There is absolutely no excuse for the chronic bumblefoot we used to see in birds. Anyone allowing a bird to get to *that* state should be banned from keeping them.

A Healthy Diet

As with any creature, including humans, a healthy diet is one of the ways to a healthy life. For the last twenty years, day-old cockerels have been easily available and for most of us they made up the bulk of our birds' diet. As stated before, there is nothing wrong with DOCs, indeed, given with other food they are excellent. But they are not good enough on their own. I know many people disagree with me over this, but I am still convinced that if they improved their diet for their birds, they would also improve their breeding.

As food has been discussed before I will not go into it again except to warn about a few possible problems that may arise. Over the last five years the number of hatcheries all over Britain has been reduced. Our own local one closed down just as Jo and I took over the Centre. Finding good supplies of DOCs is not easy and for people such as ourselves, with large collections, things can get very hard. For example, in our first year on our own, Jo and I on two separate occasions were down to one day's food supply and we didn't know where we were going to get more. Both times, having spent hours on the phone and even more hours travelling we managed, but only just. Because of that we spent £7,000 on a deep freeze and chiller unit. It then took us about three months to fill the freezer section. The week after the unit was completed and filled up, our supplier had an outbreak of disease and there were no chicks available for three months. This can happen at any time to any supplier.

With increasing imports of eggs from Europe because of the EEC, many egg producers in Britain are going out of business. It is these people who order the female chicks, thus providing us with the surplus male chicks. There is increasing demand for DOCs for new falconers, mink breeders, zoos and various other users, so it is vital for all bird of prey keepers to have other sources of different types of food available in emergencies. It is also vital to teach the birds to eat a varied diet. As already discussed, birds can become food imprints and it is no good waiting until you *have* to change their diet, which could possibly happen in the coldest of weather, before trying to get birds to eat, say mice, when they have only been used to chicks.

It is good practice to have one of the DOCs tested every now and again, as salmonella has been found in them among other problems. The odd test will give you the chance to spot possible problems before they affect your birds.

Other types of food are more expensive than DOCs, but don't you think your birds are worth it? Our quail cost from 20p to 50p each, depending on the size. You would be pushed to home produce them for less than that, and the time and trouble taken to do so would be enormous. One quail is enough for most birds until you come to the big eagles and vultures. Half a quail is enough for a small hawk or falcon such as Sparrowhawks or Merlins.

Apart from varying the food types being important, it is also very important to make sure that the food is kept hygienically. If it is to be frozen, or you buy it ready frozen, make sure that freezing has been done quickly. If large bags are put into deep freezes, the middle can take up to three or four days to freeze, giving plenty of time for bacteria to build up to dangerous levels. Food should be frozen in single layers and not packed into bags until after it is frozen solid. This makes defrosting and handling far easier as well. Never feed refrozen food, it can kill.

Deep freezes and fridges should be disinfected regularly and any other food containers as well. Food should be thawed quickly and fed quickly, not left for days. Food ledges should be cleaned once a week and be positioned out of the direct sun. Remains of food in pens should be removed as regularly as possible. Owls have to be watched during the breeding season as they will often try to store food in the nests with the eggs. Not only does this raise the risk of infection in the eggs, but if old or off food is fed to newly hatched young they will die very quickly. This again is where design of pens will count. If the food ledge has a removable surface, like a drawer, surplus and old food can be removed far more easily. Nest ledges must be easy to see into.

Many people overfeed their aviary birds. Apart from very cold spells and when feeding young, birds should never have so much food that they leave it. There is a train of thought that says don't feed birds one day a week, so that they have one day in seven when they fast. With some birds such as vultures this can and does work, but it may cause bonding problems with more aggressive birds. We don't do it here except with some of the more settled very large birds.

Be very careful with food of which you don't know the origins. As I have said, road casualties are dangerous as you never know why they have been run over. A friend of mine has just told me of a rabbit brought to a falconer for his bird, that had been ferreted. It was guaranteed not shot. The chap who caught it was telling the truth; he had not shot it. But someone else had had a go previously, the rabbit had survived and carried the shot and, when it was finally caught, the bird who ate it died. One piece of lead shot is enough to kill a bird of prey. Without any shadow of doubt, no bird of prey keeper can be too careful with the food he or she feeds to the birds.

General Hygiene

Hygiene is vitally important in lots of ways as well as in food. Gloves should be cleaned and disinfected regularly; every falconer knows how quickly they get very dirty. If you don't want to risk washing them, scrape off the dirt with a blunt knife and wipe over with a cloth. Then, with one of those small misters for indoor plants, spray on a solution of disinfectant—not too strong so that it will affect the bird—and let the glove dry out overnight before use again. We

Blyth's Hawk Eagle bred at the Centre (*Eric & David Hosking*)

have experimented a little with our gloves and one of my staff found that you can put them through the washing machine and if you dry them quickly then rub, mould and generally push them around in your hands, they will come back soft again. I make no guarantees though, it will depend on the type of leather.

Falconry bags are a positive haven for disease. How many of us have left meat in bags and come back to find all sorts of disgusting things inside. Clean them regularly, once a week. Canvas ones can be scrubbed in hot water and disinfectant, good leather ones should be lined with plastic which can be cleaned easily. They should be so clean at all times that you could put in a sandwich and feel like eating it after it has been in there for half an hour. If you could not manage to eat it, your bag is a threat to your bird.

Blocks and bow perches should be scrubbed once a week and areas where birds are regularly tethered can be sprayed with disinfectant on dry days, giving time for them to dry out before returning the birds. Baths should be filled daily for tethered birds and weekly for aviary birds. A mild solution of disinfectant can be used to clean them out, if the bath is rinsed out well afterwards.

Please remember, however, that over-use of disinfectant near birds without thorough rinsing can be dangerous.

Nest ledges in pens are wonderful places for bacteria to collect. It has been noticeable that some raptor breeders will have several good breeding seasons for up to say four years, then everything starts to go wrong. We have had several reports of this. All of them have been due to nest ledges being left uncleared for that period. After we have suggested that the whole nest ledge be removed, destroyed by fire and replaced by a new one, cleaned regularly, the breeding success has returned.

All dirty material, collected faeces, dirty nest materials, food remains, clearings from pens and the like should be put on compost heaps well away from where birds are kept or should be burned, again well away from the birds.

Never put down any rat poison near birds of prey. It is not worth the risk of poisoning a bird. If you have problems with vermin, traps should be placed *outside* pens. There is no rat or mouse poison on the market today that is safe for birds of prey.

Keep an eye on the birds' mutes. This is easy with trained birds, but not so easy with aviary birds. However, if you use a pair of binoculars and check the mutes under perches, it is surprising how much you can see. Any abnormalities should be noted and fresh samples

Blewitt, a male Lanner bred at the Centre in 1977. He is one of the best demonstration birds I have ever come across

taken to the local laboratory for testing. By the time aviary birds are showing signs of illness, the disease is probably well advanced and it may be too late. After a while, with experience, looking at the birds regularly, you may find that you occasionally just get a feeling that something is odd, not quite right. *Don't* ignore that feeling, you could well be right. Every time I have had that feeling and ignored it I have regretted it.

All these requirements of health and hygiene should be routine on the part of keepers of birds of prey. They are basic to maintaining the health, in both breeding and hunting birds.

The Sick Bird

Any sick bird should be isolated immediately in warm, quiet and dim quarters until the problem has been diagnosed. If you haven't got indoor isolation quarters you are in trouble. You should always be organised to cope with such problems *before* they happen.

Broad spectrum antibiotics are useful to have on hand and used if the bird looks as if results of tests cannot be waited for, but must be prescribed by a vet, if he is able to do so. Don't ever hand on drugs to other people. Keep them locked away, and out of reach of children. Your medicine cupboard should be dark and not too warm. Expiry dates should be checked regularly on the containers. Dispose of all out-of-date drugs safely. Do not leave them where humans or animals might find them in years to come.

Some vets may prescribe drugs suitable for poultry. These are usually administered in large quantities of drinking water. Point out that birds of prey don't drink large amounts of water and that this method is often not suitable for raptors.

Fits in birds of prey has been discussed in chapter 2. There are various reasons for fits, almost all of them are caused by some dietary deficiency or other. Any bird that has fits should be taken to a vet *immediately*. It should be fed up and not flown until the vet has given the all clear. Dietary deficiency can also cause feather plucking although another reason can be boredom particularly in skylight and seclusion pens.

The occasional bird will suffer from travel sickness, I have a Lanner who is always sick when travelling in a car, and sometimes quite severely. He looks awful and is obviously very unhappy travelling. Cure—we don't travel him. I realise that this may be difficult for anyone with only one bird that they want to hunt. However, if the bird is badly sick on the way to hunting grounds it will not fly well and will have lost valuable body fluids. It would be better to use that bird for breeding rather than subject it to the misery of car sickness. Any human who has suffered this affliction (and I am one, I still get car sick) would never willingly force it on another living creature. Never travel birds hooded if they have not cast or are liable to be sick. Always keep an eye on hooded birds while they travel.

There are still falconers who leave their birds hooded for hours at a time on a regular basis. This is not only cruel, but it is unnecessary, does not get birds tame and can be dangerous. I always feel I would like to do the same thing to those people and see how they feel after two hours of sense-deprivation. I am damn sure they would not like it.

Dead Birds

Inevitably, birds in care will die occasionally, and inevitably these deaths will not always be from old age. Therefore for the sake of future birds it is important to get a post mortem done on any bird that dies; particularly if the cause of death is unknown. Sometimes you may know how it died, but not why.

Corpses should be got to the labs within a few hours of death, preferably delivered by hand. If there is any delay, put the body in a fridge and chill. If specimens are to be sent through the post they must be well parcelled and sent First Class Letter Post, not parcel post, and marked Urgent:Pathological Specimen. All symptoms should be described, and all drugs used recorded as these will affect the outcome of the report.

If a bird dies late on a Saturday or just before a Bank Holiday (which is normal), it should be frozen and then delivered for post mortem as soon as possible after the labs have opened again. Freezing must be done as quickly as possible. The fuller the deep freeze, the slower the process. Freezing does damage the body and a full post mortem will probably not be possible.

People breeding birds of prey may well find it very helpful to have all unhatched fertile eggs looked at for problems. If this helps to hatch and rear one extra bird the following year, it should pay the costs easily.

There are several very good books that go into detail on the various diseases and problems common to all birds of prey (see Bibliography). However, the best method of defence against disease is to keep birds as clean and healthy as possible to avoid problems arising in the first place.

Wildlife and
Countryside Act 1981

7 BIRDS OF PREY
AND THE LAW

Many readers will probably know something of the ins and outs of the law. It is, however, extremely confusing and difficult to understand; hopefully this chapter will clarify it a little.

The Wildlife and Countryside Act (1981)

Our own indigenous birds, including birds of prey, are all protected by the 1981 Wildlife and Countryside Act. It is illegal to:

a) kill, injure or take any wild bird (of prey);
b) take, damage or destroy the nest of any wild bird, while that nest is in use or being built;
c) take or destroy an egg of any wild bird (of prey).

It is also illegal to:
a) disturb any wild bird (of prey) included in Schedule 1 while it is building a nest or is in, on or near a nest containing eggs or young;
b) disturb dependent young of such a bird.

Although licences have been granted to take birds of prey from the wild in Britain for falconry since 1967, 1988 was the last year that such licences were granted.

Because Britain is an EEC country, CITES is implemented here through EEC regulations. Some Appendix 2/3 species are treated as Appendix 1 (known as C1) and this applies to all birds of prey. Although many foreign species of raptors are not protected in their own countries, they come under British law when anyone wants to import them to, or export them from, Britain. A CITES permit has to be obtained before any bird of prey can be brought into or taken out of Britain. Basically what all this means is that all birds of prey, regardless of their official status in the country they come from, are regarded as Appendix 1 by our government and as such come under the laws governing birds on that list. As the lists and schedules are pretty long I am not going to list them here. You will find them in the various acts available from Her Majesty's Stationery Shops.

REGISTRATION

All captive birds of prey have to be registered with the Dept of the Environment (DoE); the only exceptions are owls and Vultures.

Although these species do not have to be registered they are still protected by various laws. Captive Secretary Birds do not have to be ringed and registered at the moment, but are not officially exempt.

A registered bird has a ring and registration document, both of which are issued by the DoE. Re-registration happens at the moment every three years. The last re-registration was September 1980, the next will be September 1993.

Just because a bird is registered and has its ring and registration document, does not mean that bird is necessarily a legal bird. If at a later date information comes to light that points to a registered bird not being a legal bird, that bird will be subject to the laws governing any illegally taken bird. Therefore, if a prospective owner is not sure of the origins of a bird, the onus is on him or her to find out, and if there is doubt, he or she should not accept the bird.

RINGS

There are at present two kinds of rings issued by the DoE. Neither is particularly good, but until there is something better, we are stuck with these. The DoE is still looking at alternative rings. These will most likely be more expensive than the existing ones and the cost will fall to us, the owners and keepers of the birds. All government rings are issued by the DoE and are individually numbered. One ring is a plastic cable-tie which is placed on a bird's leg when it is full grown. Each ring's number is prefixed with the letters UK. All registered birds of prey bred before 1983 should have these cable-ties, unless the keeper has licence to hold a bird unringed. The other is a metal closed ring (a seamless metal band), bearing its own numbers and a letter to indicate the ring size, and the letters DoE. This ring is placed on a bird's leg when it is approximately ten to fourteen days old. As the leg grows, the ring becomes too small to go over the growing foot and remains on the leg. There are certain sized rings for each species of bird that are legally acceptable.

These rings must be readable at all times. Over the years (months if you are unlucky) both the cable-tie ring and the closed ring may become illegible. If this happens, the bird automatically becomes an unregistered bird until that ring is replaced. As it is wise management practice to catch up all aviary birds at least once a year for a check up, worming and the like, rings can be checked then. New rings will have to be applied for to replace worn or lost ones.

Some birds such as some of the large eagles may have no ring, usually because large birds of prey can remove the cable-tie ring with great ease. In this case the bird will have a UR (Un Rung) number on its registration document. Any movement or sale of these birds to new owners/keepers may well be restricted. The information will be on the registration document.

Since 1983 all captive-bred registerable young raptors bred in Britain should have been close ringed with the DoE ring. There are always exceptions. A ring may come off unnoticed during the young bird's growing period in an aviary. This will have to be replaced by a cable-tie, as soon as possible. Very occasionally adult bird behaviour means that their young cannot be ringed with safety, so these young may have to be cable-tied as soon as possible. Early on there were no close rings for the large eagles so all the captive-bred ones had to have cable-ties, this problem has now been solved.

Occasionally an injury to a leg may mean that the ring has to be removed. It will have to be replaced with a cable-tie after the leg has recovered. A few birds damage themselves while trying to remove a ring. We have about three birds here that consistently injure their legs trying to do this and we have been granted licence to keep these birds unrung. They have a UR number on their registration document. All the birds that have objected to rings, in my experience, have objected only to cable-ties. We have had no bird here that has objected to the closed rings.

Any bird that should be close ringed and is not, for whatever reason, needs a special licence granted by the DoE to be able to be sold. Some people refuse to use the closed rings, preferring to cable-tie young when they leave the nest. This is very unwise, the cable-ties are not as good as the closed rings and for the bird's sake, the closed rings are safer. The DoE quite rightly does not like people refusing to assist with the legal requirements, and may well refuse to issue a sale licence.

RINGING
Registerable birds of prey, ie all except the owls, Vultures and Secretary Birds, divide into two groups for ringing at the moment—the sensitives and the non-sensitives. At the time of writing the sensitives are: Golden Eagle, Goshawk, Peregrine, Merlin, Gyr Falcon, and any hybrid where one parent is a sensitive.

When any of the six sensitives are to be ringed, either with closed rings for young birds or replacement cable-ties, the keeper applies to the DoE. The correct number of rings are sent to a DoE inspector who brings out the rings and forms, and witnesses the ringing. The forms are then signed by the keeper and the inspector and returned, by the keeper, to the DoE with the appropriate fee. New registration and replacement documents are sent out for the ringed bird or birds once the fee has been accepted and the information placed in the DoE computer.

The non-sensitives are all the rest of the registerable birds of prey.

When any of these need ringing for whatever reason, the keeper applies to the DoE for the rings and these are sent direct to the keeper, along with a form. The onus is then on the keeper to ring the birds and fill in and return the form with the correct fee to the DoE. Registration documents are then sent back in the normal way.

The bird registration part of the Wildlife and Countryside Act has been a great effort in the field of job creation. The government bird registration department now employs numerous people to cope with all the paperwork. There are also two full-time inspectors—the chief wildlife inspector and his assistant. Along with the two full-time inspectors are a number of voluntary inspectors to assist in the ringing of young sensitive species during the breeding season, and to check that the regulations are generally being obeyed by the keepers of birds of prey. An official DoE inspector carries an identity card with his or her photograph. The card is signed for the Secretary of State and dated with an expiry date.

Inspectors sent out by the DoE carry out inspections, both announced and unannounced. The Wildlife and Countryside Act says the following about inspectors in Section 7 (6):

> Any person authorised in writing by the Secretary of State may, at any reasonable time and (if required to do so) upon producing evidence that he is authorised, enter and inspect any premises where a registered person keeps any wild birds for the purpose of ascertaining whether an offence under this section is being, or has been, committed on those premises.

The meaning of that statement is fairly clear. All birds of prey, whether captive bred or not, are considered to be 'wild birds'. As yet they are not thought of as domestic birds. The section quoted is one of the parts of the act dealing with the registration of schedule 4 birds which includes birds of prey.

The act goes on to say, Section 7 (7);

> Any person who intentionally obstructs a person acting in the exercise of the power conferred by subsection (6) shall be guilty of an offence.

So, although an inspector cannot force his or her way onto your premises to inspect the bird or birds, if you intentionally refuse the inspector entry, you are breaking the law and are guilty of an offence. The inspector will then be well within his or her rights to return with the police and a search warrant should the police deem it necessary.

The DoE inspectorate have now had years to learn about not only the legal requirements, but also the problems that keepers have. They are now pretty careful about when they inspect, and respect the fact that the birds require peace and quiet during the breeding season. However, if a person is suspected of an offence, birds may well have to be disturbed during the breeding season to verify that all is well, or not well, whichever the case may be.

The words 'at any reasonable time' are most relevant to breeders of birds. At any time during the run up to, or during the breeding season, it is not a good idea to have to go into pens to catch up birds and check on ring numbers. However, if sensitive birds are being bred, they may well be subject to unannounced inspections during the breeding season, when an inspector will want to be able to view the birds to see if they are really showing signs of breeding. This is yet another reason for building good pens where viewing is easy and does not disturb the birds to any detrimental degree. However awkward it is, the phrase 'at any reasonable time' does not mean 'at the keeper's convenience'.

When an inspector makes an appointment to come over and witness the ringing of a bird or birds, remember that they are not supposed to touch the birds in any way other than to view the ring going on or perhaps visibly check the number of a ring already in position. If you know an inspector is coming to ring birds for you, have someone else on hand to help. Particularly if the ring is a cable-tie, it is very difficult to put on the cable-tie rings one handed. It is much better, and quicker, for the bird to have two people, one holding the bird and one putting on the ring. As the inspector is not supposed to handle birds, it is unfair to ask him or her to do so.

If an inspector makes an unannounced inspection and wishes to check on rings outside the breeding season, this can be extremely inconvenient and sometimes difficult, particularly with large numbers of birds. As all birds should be caught up once a year for general health and care checks, it may be worthwhile to contact the Registration Department of the DoE and inform your case officer that you intend catching up birds to do a physical check on such and such a date and would an inspector like to check the ring numbers at the same time. If you give enough notice this may be helpful to both parties.

INJURED WILD BIRDS
Anyone who finds an injured wild bird of prey is allowed to keep and look after that bird with the intention of releasing it back to the wild, unless that person has already been convicted under the Wildlife and Countryside Act. In that case, to take in an injured bird to care for it would be to commit another offence against the same Act. It would also be illegal to accept an injured bird if that person

had a court order against him stating anything to the contrary. Any injured bird of prey except the British owls must be registered immediately by the person who wishes to care for the bird. As the fee for registration varies, it is best to contact the DoE to see what it is for whichever species has been found.

If the bird cannot be released back to the wild, any person may keep that bird, unless the law disallows this for whatever reason, and the bird will then be treated as any other registerable bird, subject to the normal fees. The DoE may ask for a veterinary certificate to prove that the bird is non-releasable. There are exceptions to this regulation. Veterinary surgeons, and licensed rehabilitation keepers (LRKs) are able to accept injured wild birds of prey and care for them for six weeks without registering them. Most releasable birds will have been released during that period. If a bird has to stay with the LRK for longer than six weeks it must be registered in the normal way, as have permanently disabled birds, but the fee is waived to LRKs. Once a bird is released then the DoE is informed and the registration documents returned to them.

LRKs have to keep DoE forms and paperwork about each bird brought in to them. They are inspected to gain their initial licence and pay a three yearly LRK fee. LRKs are subject to inspections by a DoE inspector as are other keepers. The DoE asks that injured wild birds of any of these five sensitive species be reported immediately: Golden Eagle, Goshawk, Peregrine, Merlin, and Gyr Falcon.

LRKs have *no special authority* other than to have fees waived for permanently disabled birds and a six-week holding period for injured wild birds before registration. It is illegal for LRKs, or anyone else

Peregrine Falcon

for that matter, to display injured wild birds of prey to the public for financial gain, or to sell them (see page 190).

Still, I am afraid that unannounced and announced inspections are all part of the Wildlife and Countryside Act, so there is little point in getting upset and bucking the system. All that does is get falconers and bird of prey keepers a bad name and does no one any good in the long run. If both sides try to make the whole job pleasant and efficient, the effect on the birds should be minimal. If you consider that an inspector is being unreasonable immediately contact your case officer at the DoE who may ask you to explain the circumstances to the chief wildlife inspector. Try to remain calm at all times.

APPRAISAL OF THE ACT

Sadly the government system for running the civil service in general is now very outdated. It seems that as soon as someone in any governmental department gets to know and understand the system, they promptly get moved to a different job and department. Any business that was run in this way would be bankrupt very quickly. But this is the way the system works at the moment and so it has to be accepted.

I don't think anyone had any idea of what was being taken on and how many birds of prey were captive in Britain when the legislation was proposed. The initial staff put in to start the ball rolling was far too small and they must have been horrified by the prospect of trying to deal with about 10,000 birds of prey that had to be registered, and 2,000 owners who generally were not particularly keen on the idea in the first place! Mistakes have been made on both sides, sometimes justified and sometimes not. However, what must be remembered is that the DoE did not make the Wildlife and Countryside Act, they only administer it. So help them to do this as well as possible, for all our sakes.

The Act is, in my opinion, an unwieldy law and I don't think it has really made much difference to the safety of the wild populations of raptors in Britain. It has certainly made the sport of falconry very much more complicated. I, and I think a number of other falconers, believe that it would have been far better to license the falconers rather than register the birds, in much the same way as the United States regulations work. In this way, at least there would have been some sort of proficiency test before interested people were allowed to go out and buy a bird of prey, rather than the system that we have now which does nothing to protect birds that are in captivity and yet called wild, and little to protect those in the wild.

What Birds can be Sold and How

No injured wild bird of prey can be legally sold, nor can any legally taken wild bird of prey. Because all birds of prey (including owls) come under Annex C1 of the EEC CITES regulations (1982) for importing into this country, it is almost impossible to import a wild-taken bird of prey for trade. Therefore imported wild-taken birds of prey cannot be sold, except under exceptional circumstances and with a special licence.

An imported captive-bred bird might be granted a special sale licence. This would be an individual licence granted only for a particular bird and a particular person; it will have to be re-applied for should the bird be resold. It is preferred that captive birds are imported into this country for better reasons than just trade.

A number of general exemption sale and display licences granted by the DoE cover United Kingdom captive-bred birds of prey. The regulations authorise 'the display to the public for commercial purposes and the sale, keeping for sale, offering for sale and transporting for sale'.

OWLS
Barn Owl (*Tyto alba*)
Captive-bred Barn Owls may be sold if they are close ringed in accordance with the Wildlife and Countryside Act 1981, and there is documentary evidence of captive breeding. Exemption No EC CITES GEX/33. The rings must have been issued by the British Bird Council (BBC), or the International Ornithological Association (IOA).

Eagle Owl (*Bubo bubo*)
Hawk Owl (*Surnia ulula*)
Scop's Owl (*Otus scops*)
Tengmalm's Owl (*Aegolius funereus*)
The above 4 species, captive bred, may be sold without a ring, but the bird's parents must have been lawfully in captivity when the eggs were laid. Documentary evidence of captive breeding must accompany the sale. Exemption No EEC CITES GEX/33.

Tawny Owl (*Strix aluco*)
Snowy Owl (*Nyctea scandiaca*)
Little Owl (*Athena noctua*)
Short-eared Owl (*Asio flammeus*)
Long-eared Owl (*Asio otus*)
The above 5 species, captive bred cannot be sold unless a special individual sale licence is granted for individual birds.
Exemption No EEC CITES GEX/34.

All other owls captive bred in the United Kingdom may be sold if 'they are marked by means of a numbered ring or tattoo or other

distinguishing mark which uniquely establishes the ownership and origin of the specimen in question'.
Exemption No EEC CITES GEX/34.

What must be remembered is that these regulations are only valid until the end of 1992. They may be reissued the same at that time, they may be reissued completely or partly changed, they may even be revoked and new ones issued at any time. *So anyone wishing to sell or display owls should obtain these or other regulations from the DoE before proceeding further.*

DIURNAL BIRDS OF PREY
All birds that were not bred in captivity, ie imported, wild taken under licence in the United Kingdom (or injured wild birds of prey), may not be sold under any circumstances unless a special sale licence is obtained for each individual bird. That licence will only apply to one sale, any further resale of a bird must be accompanied by a new special sale licence for each individual bird each time the bird is sold.
    The general sale and display regulations divide in two groups. Those birds bred before 1983 and those bred after 1983. (1983 is when the ringing and registration part of the Wildlife and Countryside Act came into force.)

Captive bred before 1983:
Common Buzzard (*Buteo buteo*)
Honey Buzzard (*Pernis apivorus*)
Rough-legged Buzzard (*Buteo lagopus*)
Spotted Eagle (*Aquila clanga*)
White-tailed Sea Eagle (*Haliaeetus albicilla*)
Gyr Falcon (*Falco rusticolus*)
Red-footed Falcon (*Falco vespertinus*)
Hen Harrier (*Circus cyaneus*)
Marsh Harrier (*Circus aeruginosus*)
Montague's Harrier (*Circus pygargus*)
Pallid Harrier (*Circus macrourus*)
Kestrel (*Falco tinnunculus*)
Lesser Kestrel (*Falco naumanni*)
American Kestrel (*Falco sparverius*)
Hobby (*Falco subbuteo*)
Black Kite (*Milvus migrans*)
Red Kite (*Milvus milvus*)
Sparrowhawk (*Accipiter nisus*)
Osprey (*Pandion haliaetus*)
All the above 19 species may be sold if the bird is close ringed, registered correctly with the DoE and the parents were lawfully in

captivity when the egg was laid. Documentary evidence of captive breeding must accompany the sale.
Exemption No EEC CITES GEX/35.

Golden Eagle (*Aquila chrysaetos*)
Goshawk (*Accipiter gentilis*)
Peregrine (*Falco peregrinus*)
Merlin (*Falco columbarius*)
The above 4 species, if captive bred, can be sold if the bird has been close ringed; the ring must have its own legible identity number. The bird must be correctly registered with the DoE, and the parents must have been lawfully in captivity when the egg was laid. Documentary evidence of captive breeding must accompany the sale.
Exemption No EEC CITES GEX/37.

It appears that all other diurnal birds of prey captive bred before 1983 can be sold without a close ring, but the birds must have been captive bred and the parents must have been lawfully in captivity when the egg was laid. Documentary evidence must accompany the sale and the bird must be correctly registered with the DoE and ringed.
Exemption No EEC CITES GEX/36.

Captive bred after 1983:
All pure bred diurnal birds of prey captive bred after 1983 may be sold if they are ringed with a DoE close ring, or a cable-tie if the species is one of the following, according to the schedule attached to GEX/39:

Golden Eagle (*Aquila chrysaetos*)
African Hawk Eagle (*Hieraatus fasciatus spilogaster*)
Steppe Eagle (Aquila rapax nipalensis)
Tawny Eagle (*Aquila rapax*)
The birds must be correctly ringed with the specified ring and registered, the parents must have been lawfully in captivity when the eggs were laid and documentary evidence of captive breeding must accompany the sale.
Exemption No EEC CITES GEX26.

All pure bred diurnal birds of prey captive bred after 1983 but not ringed correctly have to have an individual sale licence issued for each bird, which will only cover the one sale for which that licence was granted. All first generation hybrids whose parents are listed on the Annex to GEX/39 are covered for sale and display provided they are properly close ringed and registered. All other hybrid birds require individual sale and display exemptions.

Anyone wishing to sell or display any diurnal raptors should obtain these or other relevant regulations from the DoE before proceeding further.

There are various general exemption sale licences and information sheets on the Wildlife and Countryside Act. These are all available from the DoE. I have tried to précis the law somewhat, but it is essential that whatever you wish to do with a bird that may be affected by the law, you should find out what is allowable within the law before going ahead.

Importing and Exporting Birds of Prey

It is no longer possible to import a wild-taken bird of prey with falconry the main purpose for importing. Wild-taken birds of prey can only be imported under licence if there is a very good conservation reason for doing so. Breeding projects are acceptable, if they are well run and have good reasons for existing. Extensive proof of breeding projects, experience, and aviary space for birds to be imported should accompany any application. Take my advice, write the application out properly on rough paper before filling in any forms, then type the actual form. Badly filled in forms in illegible writing do not endear anyone to the unfortunate person having to struggle with the application.

Captive-bred birds can be imported under licence but proof of the reliability of the captive breeding must be supplied. The record of some countries is somewhat dubious and importing from them may be very difficult. Birds from countries that have not signed the CITES convention are also very difficult to obtain import papers for.

To import any bird of prey, firstly there has to be a CITES import permit issued by the DoE, allowing the bird to be imported into Great Britain. Then there has to be an export permit from the country of origin. This may not be a CITES permit as some countries have only certain species of birds of prey on Appendix 1. Birds on other schedules may not necessarily require a CITES permit to export from foreign countries, although some sort of government document is necessary for import into Britain.

Once the import and export permits have been organised and are both in date, a permit must be issued by the Ministry of Agriculture. To do this, quarantine quarters have to be found or built and then passed. The Min of Ag issue an application form to fill in with the correct information. This is sent to the Min of Ag headquarters in London who then tell the local office to inspect the quarantine quarters. If these pass, the local office informs head office and a licence is issued. Part of this licence must then be sent to the exporter of the bird and the veterinary certificate on the form must be filled in by the exporting country's government veterinary department. This completed form must accompany the incoming bird.

Once a bird arrives in the United Kingdom Customs will charge VAT on the British market value of the import, regardless of the fact that this bird may have been a gift. They know the rough values and there is little point in trying to get away with a cheaper costing as it will only hold up the process and that will do the bird no good. Handling charges on the import will be charged by the airline if one is used. There are specified ports through which birds may arrive. Should an unspecified port be preferred, special written permission will have to be gained from the DoE.

If you are considering importing a bird of a species that is already being captive bred in the United Kingdom, do some serious costings first. By the time you add the possible initial cost of a bird, the freight costs, VAT and handling charges, vet bills and either quarantine costs or the cost of building your own quarters, it will probably work out cheaper to buy a captive-bred bird from the United Kingdom than to import one from abroad.

Exporting is slightly easier. The import permit from the country the bird is going to will be the responsibility of the person receiving export, however the exporter should always make sure it is in existence before sending any bird. The exporter of a bird from this country will have to apply for a CITES export permit. Some countries require a special veterinary certificate issued by them, sent over to this country and stamped by a government local veterinary inspector (LVI). For others, just a local veterinary surgeon's certificate, issued by him or her, will suffice. Travelling boxes will have to conform with International Air Travel Association (IATA) rules for containers with which to travel birds of prey.

I feel very strongly that anyone importing a bird should go out to the exporting country and make sure that all is well. In this way the bird will be shipped in the right container with the correct paperwork and will survive the trip. The only time this is unnecessary is if you know the breeder of the bird to be imported, and know that the bird will be sent over with everything in order.

Other Legislation

Dead birds of prey may not be sold unless the seller has a licence from the DoE to sell dead birds of prey. This applies to both wild and captive birds.

Eggs may not be sold unless a special licence is granted. I am told that this would, at present, only be likely if the eggs were being sold to museums.

LAWS IN FORCE
Wildlife and Countryside Act (1981)
See page 173.

Import and Export Act (1976)
Regulates the import and export of animals and birds into and out of this country; we have discussed the EEC CITES regulations 1982.

Sale of Goods Act (1979)
If someone sells a bird and it can be proved that he had foreknowledge of a problem with that bird or with that particular line of birds being bred, he or she could be taken to court.

Animal Health Act (1981)
This covers the movement of birds and animals, among hundreds of other things. If birds are travelled in a manner not deemed to be fit or kind to the bird, the keeper of that bird can be taken to court.

Criminal Justice Act (1972)
Anyone injuring or killing a bird belonging to someone else can be taken to court in contravention of this Act.

Criminal Damage Act (1971)
Does roughly the same as the above.

Police and Criminal Evidence Act (1984)
Means that land other than a dwelling house may be be entered and searched. Section 19 of the Wildlife and Countryside Act does the same thing and the police would be more likely to use the latter.

Carriage of Animals, EEC Council Directive 77/489
Deals with the protection of animals/birds during international transport.

Protection of Animals Act (1911)
Covers all cruelty to animals and birds, either direct cruelty or cruelty due to poor housing or management.

Abandonment of Animals Act (1960)
Mentioned in chapter 8.

Cruelty to Animals Act (1876)

Transit of Animals (General) Order (1973)
This covers the transporting of animals and birds, meaning they should not suffer from any unnecessary discomfort.

Veterinary Surgeons Act (1966)
This should be obtained and studied by all who are running Bird Rescue Centres, Bird Hospitals and the like.

Medicines Act (1968) and Poisons Act (1972)
These relate to the treatment of birds and the use of medications.

There are many more acts and orders and EEC directives that I have not covered, but which may well affect keepers of birds of prey. A copy of all acts can be bought from Her Majesty's Stationery Office. It is only sense to have copies of some of these acts that may well affect what you do with either falconry, breeding or injured wild birds of prey.

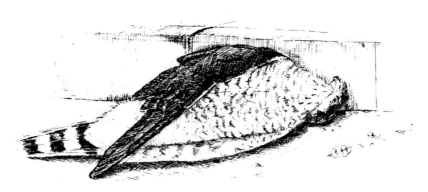

8 INJURED WILD BIRDS
OF PREY

With a greater public interest in birds of prey, many more wild birds of prey that would probably have died naturally, are found and taken to people who care for such birds for rehabilitation. More bird hospitals and sanctuaries are therefore coming into existence. Most, but not all, are started with all the right intentions and by very dedicated people. However, it is very easy for things to get out of control as the public get to hear of centres and more and more birds get brought in to be cared for. I would like people to think *very* carefully about what they are doing with injured wild birds and ask them, as I ask myself, to look very hard at each case. True conservation of the species should be the first consideration, welfare and quality of life for the individual birds the second and one's own pleasure and self gratification only last.

The NBoP Centre takes in up to one hundred injured wild birds of prey each year. The numbers have increased greatly over the twenty-two years that we have been in existence, mainly because we have become better known. It is interesting though, because it seems that one can almost tell when certain species are on the increase in the wild, by the number of injured individuals of that species brought in. All injured birds of prey are accepted here, not because we particularly wish to run a bird hospital, but because being so close to the public, it would be wrong not to accept and care for these birds, and accept the decisions for the people who bring them in.

We have had people phone up in the early hours of the morning because they have found a sick bird of prey and want to help it and don't know what to do. One lorry driver phoned late in the evening almost in tears because he had hit an owl and could not find anyone who would help him. He had been turned away by the RSPB who will not take in injured wild birds, the police who couldn't help him and the RSPCA who do normally help but had at the time got the answerphone on. He drove a hundred miles out of his way to deliver this owl at about 1am.

We and many other people who accept injured birds have numerous stories of the efforts that the British public will go to to help injured wildlife. And I get a great feeling of pride to live in a country with so many people who will put themselves out to such a degree. It also shows a rising concern in conservation, which is very pleasing. Many people get so interested they will phone again to see how the bird is getting on. But, for those people who accept these birds and care for them, common sense and kindness should come *before* overriding feelings of, sometimes misplaced, affection.

Now I know that some of the statements I am going to make in this chapter will upset some people and will make me appear very uncaring for injured wild birds of prey. This is definitely not true. There are few people now caring for birds of prey who were literally brought up from the cradle with them, taught from a very early age to care for and respect wildlife in general and birds of prey in particular, as I was. As I have said before, they are so much a part of my own life that they come before everything else, as can be seen by the style of life I lead. I have never been able to physically kill a bird of prey, that is either hit it on the head or throw it against a wall as some vets suggest as a form of euthanasia. I once had to shoot a horrifically injured baby Tawny Owl as it was the only method of killing it quickly that I had to hand, and that I could summon up the courage to manage. I have never forgotten it and can describe it vividly to this very day, eleven years on. I don't think that anyone can justly accuse me of not caring. But there is a vast difference between caring and over sentimentality.

There are some people who will save the life of an injured bird regardless of the resulting quality of life. Anyone seriously wanting to care for injured wild birds cannot afford to be self indulgent, but should care for the birds never forgetting the state of the species in the wild and the possible state of the individuals in care. Nor should it be forgotten that there are laws protecting wild birds, injured or otherwise (see chapter 7).

It should always be realised that surviving as a wild creature is very hard. Wild birds of prey live much shorter and more hazardous lives than those in captivity. The natural mortality rate for wild birds of prey can be as high as 50 per cent or higher. This means that 50 out of every 100 young born in some species may be dead before the end of their first year. This is perfectly normal; 50 per cent surviving each year is enough for the species to continue. It is most likely the birds in the 50 per cent that weren't going to make it, are the ones that will be found and brought to Licensed Rehabilitation Keepers (LRKs), or the like, for care and treatment. The chances of many of those birds surviving after being treated and returned to the wild are very slim. Many of them have already proved their unfitness for survival by being found injured and brought in, in the first place. This is of course not always the case, but in a very high percentage it is so. Although many birds get hit by cars, very often these accidents occur after a spell of hard weather when the bird, not in top condition and becoming weaker through unsuccessful hunting, is not quick enough to get out of the way of a vehicle. Very often these birds would have died anyway had they not been hit.

What I am trying to say is that a certain amount of hardness of heart should be employed when dealing with injured wildlife. If birds of a common species are brought in with *severe* injuries, there is no good conservation reason for keeping them alive. For example, one-winged Kestrels can and do live a long time in captivity. They will also breed in captivity but, as discussed in chapter 5, there is little use for numerous young Kestrels, either in falconry or in the wild. For every more common permanently disabled bird kept, there is likely to be less space for an injured bird that could be cared for and be a valuable contribution to its species either by being returned to the wild or, if that is not possible, by being used for captive breeding.

There are no colony-living species of birds of prey native to Britain. All our wild birds live either in pairs or, in many of our species, as individuals spending a good part of their lives on their own. Keeping large numbers of one species of permanently disabled birds together in one pen indefinitely, to save space, rather than more naturally in pairs, is not particularly kind to the birds. No one can really quantify the stress this puts on them.

So, if you look after injured wild birds of prey already or are thinking of doing so, for the sake of the individual birds, the sake of others that may come in and the sake of the species, don't hang on to one-legged, one-winged, blind or otherwise crippled birds just to gratify your own feelings. Care for everything as well as possible, but don't be so soft hearted that you can't humanely have put to sleep birds that should not survive and which, if they hadn't been found, most definitely would not have survived.

Using just one species and a hypothetical calculation, a little sum will point out what sort of numbers may die quite naturally in the wild and what sort of numbers keepers might have to look after if every permanently disabled bird was kept. Imagine 100,000 Kestrels living in Great Britain, giving say 40,000 possible pairs. Say 25,000 of those possible pairs bred and reared to flying age 2.5 young per brood; there could be 62,500 young kestrels flying around in July. If 70 per cent were destined not to survive, the total number of young

Kestrels that would die or get injured and then die, in one year would be 43,750. That doesn't even count any of the adult birds.

If only 5 per cent of of that 70 per cent were found and brought in, there would be 2,187 Kestrels to care for, which is an awful lot of birds found and brought in. You can see why it is so important for only those birds which have a high chance of surviving to be released and why it is best not to keep all the rest in captivity as the numbers over just a few years would be simply horrific. If 50 per cent of those Kestrels could be released, the other 50 per cent kept alive and cared for by LRKs, each bird living 15 years and presuming that approximately the same number was kept each subsequent year, the number of disabled Kestrels being housed, fed and cared for by the end of those 15 years would be 16,402, and the money and time spent to look after them enormous.

Although those figures are only hypothetical, it is nevertheless easy to imagine the problem and also easy to see why rehabilitators should be hard to be kind and be selective about those permanently disabled birds destined to be kept for the rest of their natural lives.

DISPLAY OF INJURED WILD BIRDS

I am afraid that there are at the moment a few people taking injured wild birds of prey to country fairs and shows, and displaying them to the public to gain sympathy and funds. I believe this is morally very wrong. Injured wild birds, recovering, should be left quietly in pens prior to release. Permanently disabled birds (if they are going to be kept) should be allowed to live out their lives in peace, not dragged round the country in boxes and displayed for the public, even for the reason of fund raising. Any necessary fund raising can be very successful if done using photographs and explanations, not live injured wild birds.

In the last year I have seen a number of injured wild birds displayed in very poor conditions at various shows, being handled and stroked constantly by visiting children and adults, in even the hottest weather. We have about sixty-five species of birds here at the Centre, totalling about 220 birds and although some of them will tolerate being stroked, *none* of them, with the exception of an imprinted, tame Caracara, enjoy being touched. Constant stroking of birds is very bad for feather condition, as it removes all the natural oil which cannot be replaced fast enough.

Not only is all this exposure unpleasant for the individual birds, but it does the sport of falconry no good and puts LRKs into a bad light. Being an LRK myself I object to that, and am sure that most other reputable LRKs would feel the same. Discerning members of the public at these shows have come to me and been very upset by these sorts of displays, and the conditions in which the birds have been presented. I hope that the recent letter sent round by the DoE informing LRKs that the display of injured birds for financial gain is illegal, will stop this. Only those with the suitable charitable status or with zoo licences will be able to continue this behaviour, and I hope that they will have the decency not to do such a thing.

Requirements for Care

However, to get away from some of the more negative aspects of injured birds of prey, there is no doubt that some very valuable work has been, and is, being done with injured wild birds of prey. As Andrew Greenwood discussed in a paper in 1977, the role that could be played by bird hospitals in monitoring the diseases of wild species could be very important. We have learnt a great deal in techniques, particularly as regards coping with broken limbs which are far more plentiful in injured wild birds than in captive ones. Starvation and dehydration are things that are not normally dealt with in captive populations, but are probably the most common problem with wild birds. So much can be learnt which could then be applied to saving rare and endangered species.

There are seven major requirements for anyone wishing to look after injured wild birds of prey:

1 A good and patient vet
2 Recovery facilities
3 Land for pens
4 A good and varied supply of food
5 Time
6 Money
7 Release sites

A GOOD VET

Many injured birds will require veterinary treatment, particularly if they have broken limbs, even if they only need an X−ray to check for breaks. Although the College of Veterinary Surgeons has suggested to all vets that they treat injured wild birds free of charge, many of them don't. To be fair to the vets, it is costly treating injured birds and many just can't afford to give their services free. We are very lucky; one of our vets looks after all the injured birds brought to us free of charge. If he and his associates didn't do this for us, we would not be able to afford the sort of treatment many of these birds require.

Firstly, find out if you have a local vet who is willing to treat injured wild birds of prey. Make sure that even if he or she is not experienced with these birds of prey, they have access to vets that are, and use that access. See if you are going to be charged for the treatment of injured wild birds. If so, it would be advisable to get a rough estimate of the charges for various forms of treatment—the cost of an X—ray, the cost of an operation to set a broken limb, the cost of drugs etc. All these will give you an idea of the sort of bill to expect for each bird. It may also be one of the deciding factors in which bird gets what treatment. Euthanasia is best performed by a vet as well.

RECOVERY FACILITIES

These are the next thing required for injured birds. Three different types of accommodation, and a storage room, are needed to do the job properly:

Small box-type quarters to confine birds for initial monitoring, recovering from operations and anaesthetics, or confinement for other reasons.

Larger, room-type accommodation, for birds that need a little more space but may also require heat, or are not ready to go into outside pens.

Large outside pens or flights where birds can fly about to aid recovery and muscle tone, or for housing growing young birds of prey which need to have space to learn to fly.

The small boxes should be in a building or room that is fairly light, but does not have too much direct sunlight. A couple of the boxes should be dark or dim, the rest should have single opening doors with vertical bars to let in light and air. The room should be heatable but should be well ventilated and not get over hot during summer. The boxes should be lined with some material which is easy to keep clean.

The boxes in our sick quarters are lined in white china tiles. These are very nice to wash as long as they are cleaned every day. The perches are removable and covered in carpet which can be replaced regularly. The bars on the doors are either bamboo or hollow aluminium tubing. The floor of each box is covered with clean newspaper each day; if a bird needs a softer surface, a towel is placed in the box. The room has a concrete floor which is easy to wash and the door has a panel which opens to give extra ventilation is hot weather. The windows open and the inside frames are covered with vertical bars.

It is a good idea to have a container for water in each box, one which will not tip over. Sick birds should always have the opportunity to drink and birds on antibiotics will often wish to drink, as some antibiotics can have a dehydrating effect.

The larger rooms are pretty basic, well lit and ventilated, quiet, draught proof, heatable and easily cleaned. We cover the floor in sand and put in branches as perches which are replaced each time the room is used. A double door system is vital.

The outside pens should be sheltered, and if not in total seclusion, part of each pen should be secluded, so the birds can get out of sight of humans. Wild Goshawks will have to go into total-seclusion pens. Plenty of light, plenty of shelter, lots of room and lots of peace and quiet are the most important needs. The RSPCA Wildlife Unit use a large swinging perch which Paul Llewellwyn at Swansea University researched and found very useful in helping birds recover balance and muscle after injury.

The pens should be kept clean and free of undergrowth, with plenty of perches for recovering birds to use. Again the double door system is essential (see chapter 4).

A room with deep freezes for storing food, a fridge, a cupboard with bandages and standby medicines, a treatment table, weighing machine, gloves, clean newspaper, spare pieces of carpet, clean perches, spare boxes for travelling birds, brooms, mops, disinfectant and the like, is essential.

LAND FOR PENS

Plenty of space, in a large garden or field that is secure, will be required, as the pens should be well away from noise, dogs, people etc. It is surprising how much space can be taken up by even a few pens. The area put aside for building pens should be dry and airy, not under trees where it will be dark and damp for much of the year.

Our new tile-lined sick quarters

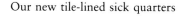

GOOD, VARIED FOOD SUPPLY

At certain times of the year, particularly towards the end of the breeding season when larger numbers of young may be brought in, a good food supply is vital. Young birds of prey go through large quantities of food during the growing period. It is very important to feed them on more than one food type so as to avoid food imprints (the fixing of a bird onto one food type only). Some sort of food that looks similar to the food they will be catching on their return to the wild must be provided so that they know what to look for when hunting. The number of fluffy, yellow, day-old chicks wandering about in the wild is decidedly limited.

TIME

Time is probably the most unpredictable factor; there will be times when few or even no injured birds come in, and others when they arrive almost by the score. Once a place is known for taking injured birds, they will arrive at all hours of the day and night. We have phone calls about injured birds as late as midnight and this can get irritating after years of it happening. We very rarely go out and collect birds, we worked out recently that if we still did so now, we would have one member of staff on the road, full time, for nearly six months of the year. But we do accept birds at any time if they are delivered to us.

The amount of time the birds take will, of course, vary with the number of birds brought in and the degree of care each one needs. However, time *will* be needed, and quite considerable amounts of time, on occasion. If you are liable to be short of this, or want such luxuries as holidays, then coping with injured wild birds, other than just the very occasional one, is not for you.

MONEY

Housing, feeding, treating and caring for injured wild birds of prey is expensive. The recovery facilities are probably the single largest capital outlay, if they are done well.

Personally, I see no point in taking on such a responsibility if it is not done well. I also think it is much better if facilities are built attractively and to last. Why build a tatty eyesore; it does not endear bird keepers, falconers or LRKs to their neighbours, nor does it promote any feelings of professionalism in those people who bring in birds. A nice, tidy, smart, clean set of buildings will engender feelings of pride in the owner and feelings of relief in the people who find and deliver these birds. It will also make the care of these birds much easier. But good buildings are expensive to put up, so money must never be left out of the plans to care for injured birds.

Food, lighting, heating, possible vet bills and medicaments will all add to the bills. Don't try valuing your time or you will get most depressed!

RELEASE SITES
The aspect often forgotten in the treatment and care of injured wild birds of prey is suitable release sites when the birds have recovered sufficiently. Please note that I say 'suitable'. There is too much haphazard releasing of birds of prey. We do not release birds from here, at least none that need any form of hacking back (a slow release using pens and food or falconry methods). We do not consider that this is a suitable place from which to hack birds, so all our injured wild birds of prey go on to people who have good available release sites and can manage to release the birds successfully.

Also note the words 'recovered sufficiently'. Once a wild bird comes in injured, it comes under certain laws preventing cruelty to animals. If a bird is released and it could be proved that it was not sufficiently recovered to survive, or had been released in an unsuitable area, the person releasing that bird can be taken to court under the Abandonment of Animals Act 1960. So be careful to make sure that birds are ready to go and are released in suitable areas (see page 200).

Accepting and Treating

When we receive a phone call about a bird, we first of all see if it is in the hand or the bush, so to speak. If it is still loose in the wild (as many of them are) we tell people to try and catch up the bird and then phone us again after having done so. You have no idea how many supposed injured birds turn out to be extremely healthy, when people try to catch them. In the days when we did go out to collect them, it was fairly common to have a bird fly off either before we got there or just as we arrived. I once drove a round total of thirty miles to catch a 'giant eagle with an injured leg' only to find a perfectly fine heron, standing on one leg, which then stood happily on both its legs prior to flying off.

Normally an injured bird is relatively easy to catch, by cornering and dropping a lightweight coat or large towel over it. And people get very pleased with themselves if they have succeeded in catching one. If the bird is obviously a trained bird, we try to send out someone with a lure to pick it up.

We first ask if the bird is injured and we have various standard questions that we ask to try and find out what the bird is—size, eye colour, body colour etc. These are not foolproof by any means and we have had an interesting variety of very unusual 'birds of prey' brought in. One lady insisted we come out to catch a very weird-looking injured bird of prey which turned out to be a French Partridge. Several times we have had baby eagles brought in, usually in a huge cardboard box. On opening the box, you struggle to see anything in there, let alone an eyass eagle; then, hiding in a corner like a piece of dirt, you spot movement which turns out to be a young swallow or swift. They are usually mistaken because of their hooked talons which they use for clinging onto walls. I think our most exciting arrival came when someone phoned and said that they had found a baby Dodo. We thought our luck was in—the finding of an extinct bird in a country it didn't even live in—our fortune was made. It turned out to be a baby Wood Pigeon, right family but wrong species. Taking in birds is always interesting if very hard work.

We suggest placing all injured birds in a strong, dark cardboard box with an old towel or piece of carpet in the bottom. Under no circumstances use those wire cat boxes that are often used by the RSPCA . They are the last thing to use for birds in general with the possible exception of a cage made out of chicken wire, which is even worse. Old budgie cages should not be used either. A dark box will stop a bird from crashing around, damaging feathers and perhaps injuring itself further. I am glad to say that I think the RSPCA are going to stop using these boxes for birds.

Unless the bird is very weak, we suggest it is best not to feed it, particularly if it is being brought in immediately. If the finders are unable to bring round an injured bird until the following day, we suggest feeding with raw beef or chicken but not anything else. We always try to remember to tell people not to give any bird found, bacon or salted meat of any description. We have had several birds arrive that would probably have survived had they not been given a good feed of bacon before coming to us. We also point out that giving owls cotton wool as casting material is not only a complete waste of time but can often kill the birds. Casting can be traumatic and is not necessary for injured birds or young ones until they are recovered or nearly grown, whichever the case may be, as long as the food supplied is good quality.

During the spring and early summer many young birds of prey, particularly owls, are found by the walking public. If these young have only just been found and are not tiny babies, but half grown—the normal size they are when they start to get adventurous —and are obviously not injured in some way, try to persuade the people who have found the bird to return it immediately to the place where it was found. The parent birds will most likely return and care for the baby, and its chances of long-term survival are as great

A young Snowy Owl. It is very unlikely that one of these will be found in the wild in Britain

if not greater than they would be if the bird is brought in, reared and then hacked back. What is often forgotten is that young owls cannot learn to fly in their nest in a hole, they leave the nest before they can fly and practise wing flapping and pouncing and the like. If left alone they will very often climb trees long before they can fly and the parents are perfectly used to finding their young offspring in various different places.

Always thank people for bringing birds and for phoning, even if the bird is not a bird of prey. Remember, one day it could be a falconry bird that you or someone else has lost. If people recover birds that we have lost, or help us to find them, we always give a reward. This encourages help in the future.

Each bird that arrives in should have its own card with details of species, sex, age (this often has to be guessed), name and address of finder, and details of where the bird was found and under what circumstances. If the bird has obviously been shot the DoE must be informed immediately. As the bird is treated, details of the treatment and the results should be kept. This is valuable information that could be very useful at a later date.

On arrival, birds should be examined for injury, and problems noted. Shock is one of the biggest killers of wild birds, particularly haggard birds (adults). So unless treatment is needed immediately we recommend placing birds in a small, comfortable warm (but not too warm) dark box for about twelve hours before excessive handling or operating on.

Many birds, particularly those brought in during the autumn may well be on the point of starvation. This is quite common, and these birds usually come from the vast number of unsuccessful young that are failing to hunt for themselves and are doomed not to make it.

If the bird is unable even to stand, the chances of its survival are very slim. However, a multi-vitamin injection with some B vitamins, and some IonAid given orally may help the bird. It is almost impossible to give too much liquid, so with very weak birds we may give fluids such as IonAid very regularly; 4 per cent of the bird's body-weight every 4 to 6 hours will do. Food should not be given to very thin birds until the fluids have given them a little strength. They will not be able to digest solid food immediately and it will only go off in the crop, causing more problems. With these birds, Brand's Essence (beef or chicken), Ovigest or Complan can be be used in small and frequent feeds, until the bird is stronger. Once the bird is strong enough to eat, or be force fed, feed only small amounts. Little and often is the best way. Check that small crops have been put over before giving more food. With owls, who have no crops, the stomach can be gently pressed to see if quantities of food remain. If the bird regains enough strength to start feeding on its own, the battle is almost won, but again do not overfeed and don't give any casting materials until the bird is strong again; it just wastes valuable space and energy. (Casting material is fur or feathers which are eaten by the bird and subsequently regurgitated after the bird has digested its meal.)

Probably the most difficult birds to get to feed on their own are the haggard birds and particularly musket Sparrowhawks. We find that either a fresh starling or perhaps a quail which looks close to their natural food, will start them off. The less natural looking foodstuffs such as day-old chicks and white mice can be introduced if need be.

Birds with broken limbs or suspected breaks should be X-rayed by a vet and then the limbs set if need be. If the bone is holding in place (natural splinting), which may happen if only one bone in a wing is fractured, operating need not be done, just immobilise the wing. If not, pinning is probably the most successful way for birds, the bones held in place while healing proceeds.

Birds that are just ill, rather than injured can be a great problem. They should really be isolated in case they are carrying any contagious disease. Mute samples should be taken as soon as possible, taken to the Poultry Laboratories or your vet, and should the results prove the bird has a contagious disease, for the sake of other birds it is probably wiser to put the bird down, unless it is a particularly rare bird. For those people with their own breeding or falconry birds as well as injured birds, it is sheer madness to risk an infected bird close to healthy stock. If the infection is curable and not contagious, use the drug suggested on the mute sample report, after checking with your vet. Be careful not to go ahead without his say so; some poultry labs may unknowingly suggest the use of drugs which are actually poisonous to raptors.

There will be times when birds come in that have either been illegally taken as very young birds and then lost or released, or found as a very young bird by people who insist on rearing it themselves, only bringing the bird to an LRK after it has become full grown. In both cases the bird is most likely to be an imprint of some sort. Sexually imprinted birds cannot and must not be released to the wild. They will not breed, they may well attack humans if they get hungry or later on when they come into breeding condition. They will not pair up naturally, but may take over a territory and keep off a wild breeding pair that should be there. The sexually imprinted bird will either have to be kept for its natural life in a pen on its own as it will attack other birds; found a home for, making sure that the person having the bird knows what he or she is getting and knows how to cope with it; or it will have to be put down humanely.

Some birds may have been fed on only one food type and have got wedded to it, refusing to eat other foods, almost to the point of starvation. These must be slowly weaned off and encouraged to eat a variety of alternative food types.

Many injured and sick birds that come in have The NBoP Centre's favourite parasite—hipposcids, or flat fly which looks like a flat, grey house-fly, and lives in among the feathers on birds and is a blood sucker. Sometimes young birds will have an excessive number of these little delights and they will actually kill the host bird. If you see them, the bird will have to be sprayed. In fact it is a good idea to spray all birds once they are over the shock period. *Never* spray indoors. Use Alugan spray or Johnson's Antimite and, holding the bird in the fresh air well away from you, spray well. Don't hold the spray so close that the bird gets wet; don't forget to spray under the wings and tail but be careful of the eyes. Try to get to the back of the neck where feather mites love to live. The hipposcids then have a great habit of flying off the sprayed bird onto the nearest possible living thing—you. They are very difficult to kill, resisting normal fly swatting like a relation of the Incredible Hulk. You have to roll them between finger and thumb like a flea. I have known members of staff here, strip off in front of the visitors if they spot a flat fly landing on them!

Swallows, swifts and house martins have them in quantities and they will often fly onto our demonstration falcons in high summer when the house martins fly along with the falcons. Injured Merlins and Hobbys are often crawling with the damn things. Birds carrying large numbers of external parasites will often be weakened and can die. Various mites and ticks can be carried and all should be watched for.

One of the commonest injuries we seem to have with Little Owls is loss of use of their legs. Get any of these birds X-rayed first, X-raying the pelvis as well as the legs. We have found that very often the pelvis is broken, thus causing the paralysis. If the bones are uninjured let the bird recover from the shock, let any excessive bruising—which will show as green or blue skin—subside and then give the bird regular physiotherapy, bicycling the legs gently at least twice a day for ten minutes. This can and does bring back the use of the legs. If the pelvis is fractured it may eventually recover on its own but if it is badly broken, the bird's chances are slim and it is probably kinder to relieve it of its pain and have it put down.

Releasing or Hacking Back

Sometimes birds are brought in that have only had a minor knock, and by the time they arrive, are fully recovered and can be released immediately. If possible always release the bird back where it was found, or as close to that area as you can. If it has been brought a long distance and cannot be returned to the area of finding, release the bird in the nearest available suitable area. If releasing a diurnal bird of prey, an early morning release is best. If releasing a nocturnal bird, release at twilight, just before full dark; in this way it will not get mobbed badly by crows and the like.

Full-grown birds that have only had short-term treatment—up to ten days in captivity—should be able to be released without any recourse to hacking techniques, unless it is very obvious that the bird is only just full grown and has not yet caught anything. Again it is best to release as near as possible to the finding site and again, choose good weather. Don't let birds go during heavy rains or a sudden freeze.

Late summer is the very best time for releases, although autumn and early winter, depending on the weather can also be reasonable. At these times birds can be released in areas occupied by others of the same species, as this is the time of year when young are moving around, and the established pairs will not be defending their territories. During the spring and early summer, release sites must be found away from close resident pairs, or these will drive away released birds. They may even be driven away themselves, possibly resulting in the death of wild young birds that they may have been rearing. Mid-winter is a bad time to release birds, as their chances of survival in poor or freezing weather conditions are lowered. The weather forecast should be obtained from the local Meteorological Office for the following week and if strong winds or heavy rain are imminent birds should not be released at hack sites.

Suitable release sites are absolutely vital. Birds must be released in sites where they have a high chance of survival. There is no point in releasing birds such as Common Buzzards from a back garden. I really think that urban sites cut down birds' chances as there are so many possible hazards about such as traffic, cats, dogs, children, glass windows and many other problems. The birds stay here until they can be removed safely and then go to West Hotel. This takes some of the work off us and means we can still accept injured birds. We send all our injured birds down to the RSPCA Wildlife Unit, West Hatch, Taunton, Somerset. They have just built new facilities and have about 20 acres (8ha) of ground, giving plenty of space for recovery pens. They also have a number of release sites spread around and about six counties, thus giving the birds the highest chance possible. Hack sites should be chosen for:
- Good habitat.
- Good food base.
- As little disturbance as possible.
- Someone available to monitor the birds' progress.
- Freedom from natural hazards such as motorways.

If there is no good wild food supply, you might just as well hit the birds on the head to avoid them starving to death slowly. A survey of the prey base should be taken before choosing a site. There should be no resident conspecific species. If you wish to release Kestrels, don't release them close to wild Kestrel territory; release something else in that area and similarly for other species.

According to the research done by P.J. Llewellwyn and P.F. Brain, mobbing by other birds can place great stress on new releases. The worst offenders are the corvids. So don't choose a release site in close proximity to a rookery or the local crows' nests, as these birds will keep newly released birds constantly on the move, taking them away from the release sites. Collapsible cages which can easily be moved to new release sites and erected are very useful, as release sites must not be over used, with over-high numbers released.

For release of young birds back to the wild it seems that group releases of four or five birds together are more successful. Once they have settled in the release pen (not to be confused with a pheasant release pen) and can be let out, small groups together will tend to keep one another close to the food supplied by the attendant until they get more adventurous. Sometimes released birds may decide to take up residence in the hack area and start to breed, in which case no more of that species can be released there and a new area will have to be found. Take heart though, that is a sign of success.

●No bird that is not physically and structurally perfect should be released.
●No bird that has damaged feathers should be released. Unless that damage is very minor.
●No bird imprinted on humans should be released.
●No bird that is not fit should be released.

In cases where birds have been under treatment for extended periods, often the only way to assess fitness is to use falconry methods and train and fly the birds prior to release.

All birds should be ringed by the British Trust for Ornithology (BTO) before release. Ring returns will show the success of many releases and are a valuable contribution to conservation work. I spoke to Colin Seddon, who runs the Wildlife Unit near Taunton, and he said that he has found feeding live food to birds was not necessary prior to release. He has ring returns from Tawny Owls that have been out for three years successfully and they were brought to the unit as 7-day-old babies. None of his release birds are given live food.

Talking about baby Tawnies, you may well get people who have found them and phone for advice, but refuse to bring the bird in to a rehabilitation centre because they want to rear it themselves. This is understandable but you must point out politely and firmly, without being unpleasant, that the bird will not be a normal, happy, well adjusted bird if reared on its own. To keep a young bird isolated and not let it join others is self indulgent and does not have the bird's best interests at heart. If someone has been warned that to hang onto a bird unnecessarily will render it non-releasable by imprinting it, they could be deemed to be breaking the law if they persist.

There are hundreds of very dedicated people who take in and look after wildlife all over the world. They do a vital and worthwhile job. All I would ask of some of them, and anyone considering starting a bird hospital, is think about what they are doing, and why they are doing it.

9 IS IT FOR YOU?

There are many reasons for owning or wanting to own animals or birds, some far easier to explain that others. Man has caught and in many cases domesticated wildlife for thousands of years. It is very much a part of our evolution and history. I know of no culture, worldwide, that does not keep some sort of animal as 'pets', albeit that they may be eaten in hard times. For some humans it is the only way they can communicate with another living thing. For many of us, life without the physical presence of living things other than humans would be intolerable.

There is something very special about birds of prey. They have fascinated humans for centuries, and I can well understand what draws certain people to them and to falconry, even though I accepted them so naturally, being born and brought up with them. They are without doubt very beautiful and fly superbly. Perhaps part of the attraction is because raptors are hunters and mankind is still very much a hunter. So to watch raptors hunting has, for many people, a particular interest.

Birds of prey have a long history with man. Falconry is possibly four thousand years old and the relationship that one has with a bird is very special and totally different from that with a domestic animal such as a dog. Dogs fit in with man, usually trying to please him. Raptors are far more independent. Much as I love my birds and know them well, I don't think they would pine if I dropped dead tomorrow, but my dogs would definitely miss me. Yet when a dog comes when called, it is not so special as when a bird comes back. I suppose it's the element of air that makes the difference, or part of it. If the dog doesn't come you can eventually chase it and catch it, but unless you can fly, you can chase a bird all day, end up very bad tempered and still not get airborne.

As with all outdoor and indoor pastimes, falconry is becoming increasingly popular. But not all those entering it are learning the techniques *before* getting a bird, and many don't realise the long-term commitment that is required to do the birds, and the sport, justice. This is starting to cause problems. Some think that falconry is what they have seen from a flying demonstration, which may well have been a poor one. The trouble with such a demonstration is that, done well, the birds should fly well and the whole thing look very easy—unfortunately it looks much too easy for those who fancy trying it themselves.

People with sporting dogs who have watched well trained dogs in gundog and obedience tests, will know the problems when trying to get their own dogs to behave even half as well, and the same thing goes for birds. Falconry demonstrations are *not* falconry, they are just a demonstration of some of the training methods with, one hopes, necessarily first-class birds. The difference between them and falconry itself is like the difference between a gundog demonstration and going out on a good shoot with your dog to point or pick up. They are worlds apart.

One of the biggest worries with inexperienced people trying to train birds is when things start to go wrong. And this is also the time when a falconry book tends to be not a lot of use. With dogs and horses (and humans), if the training goes wrong, in most cases you just end up with a badly behaved one of whichever it is. If things go wrong in training birds of prey the mistakes will probably result in the death of the bird. It is very easy to kill a bird with inexperience and very easy to lose one which is not ready to fend for itself.

Using books as sole reference is definitely not the way to learn falconry. As an aid to falconry they are vital if they are good, but I think that at the moment the only sensible and responsible way to learn the techniques of falconry in this country is to go on a reputable falconry course. In this way you can find out if you are the right person to have a bird, see if you really have the patience to cope with it and learn about most of the problems, the amount of time needed and all the techniques in handling and training a bird without harming or killing it. The only other alternative in Britain is to try to find a good falconer who has the time and the inclination to teach you. They are hard to find. Few people have the time to give to beginners, or may not have the talent to pass on their knowledge. If you can't afford the time or expense to go on a course, you certainly can't afford to take up falconry because it is both time consuming and expensive.

Because The NBoP Centre has been established for such a long time and is readily available to people who think they want to start falconry, we tend to see most of the problems that can be encountered. I suppose that is why I have written this book. As so often stressed

already, I believe it is very important to ask anyone planning on taking up the sport of falconry, trying to captive breed or just keeping
birds, to think before they do it. To be quite frank, I would like some
people who are already involved to look at what they are doing and
how they are doing it, and perhaps change things a little.

There are very few people who can fly more than one bird and
give the flying time to do it or themselves justice, particularly with
hawks and buzzards. In fact I would go as far as to say that 95 per
cent of birds flown in this country are not fit, not by a long way. In
this I am not even counting birds owned by the 'Robin Hood falconers'
who don't even fly their birds but pose with them instead, perhaps
wandering around at shows where they know there is going to be a
falconry demonstration, or taking them to the pub. Far more people
would have excellent birds if they flew one bird well, at least four
times a week and preferably more, thus giving the bird the chance
to get fit and therefore confident.

When flying falcons, more than one can be flown, although even
those who are lucky enough to have permission to fly over grouse
moors and can take several falcons to hunt with, are pushed to fly
more than three birds well. Those who have and take up to seven
birds are just downright greedy in my opinion and I would be very
surprised if any of their birds are of good quality. And yet there is
at the moment quite a large number of private people keeping well
over the number of birds that could possibly be flown well. Many
of them are kept tethered, not even with the chance of breeding.
This puts pressure on falconry. There is no way I can justify anyone
keeping a bird tethered if it is not being flown. There are already a
number of groups who are starting to attack falconry, along with
other forms of hunting and keeping animals, such as the zoos which
they already target. Keeping excessive numbers of birds without a
valid reason is perfect ammunition to those groups. I am getting more
and more aware of the numbers of societies who are jumping on the
bandwagon to stop humans from keeping any wildlife in captivity.

All this may be a little hypocritical coming from someone
who has over two hundred birds here. It certainly sounds bloody
hypocritical. But please remember that The NBoP Centre has been
in existence since 1966. The birds are here to do a very different job
from the normal falconer's bird. They are public relations people
for their own species, teaching the general public about raptors and
conservation. At the same time they lead a very valuable existence
breeding in captivity, thus giving us far greater insight into the birds
and hopefully ensuring their future. With the help of dedicated staff,
we fly up to thirty birds a day during the summer months. However
when it comes to falconry rather than demonstration work, I and my
staff only have one hunting bird each, if that.

All the birds here at the Centre have a purpose, either breeding, demonstration work or hunting. If a bird is not needed here for any of those jobs, or cannot fit in with our way of life, it is offered to others who may be able to do it more justice than we can. The only exceptions are those birds who have served us for many years either flying or breeding and who are now too old for the job. These retire with us here.

I am sad to say that this is not always so with others. I know of a case where a Peregrine, imported seventeen years ago and who had, one can only assume, outlived its usefulness, was released out into the wild to fend for itself. The bird was found and brought to us. It had bumblefoot which it had obviously had for some considerable time, and one useless toe. As I was told roughly when it had been released, it was pretty clear to me that these injuries were with the bird before that. He was close to starvation, dehydrated, exhausted and generally pretty ill. He stayed with us for several days and then, against my better judgement he was returned to his owner. I don't

A very sick and elderly
Peregrine, who should
have been lovingly
retired

know if the bird survived, I can only hope so, for I have not been informed. One can only hope that the person in question does not do the same thing to his family in their old age.

As with a dog, your bird should be for life.

The forces against keeping any living creature in captivity are growing all the time. It is important to keep an open mind and try to understand why this is happening and try to see the other point of view.

I don't believe that it is wrong to have animals in captivity, or I would not be doing what I do. Birds of prey, if kept properly, certainly take to captivity very well. If each individual bird is well looked after, if the wild population is not affected by having members of its species in captivity and if there is a good reason for having these birds then who am I, or anyone else, to say that it shouldn't be done.

Each falconer or breeder or keeper of birds of prey is, however, at all times a public relations man for his hobby and should always remember this when handling birds particularly when he may be seen by others. Always take time to answer questions politely without being too encouraging. Don't do things like feeding day-old cockerels on the fist in front of people; it does not endear raptors to those members of the public who are far less used to seeing a bird eat meat than you are.

When people phone us wanting a bird our first concern is why do they want it. Some callers name the species, sex and age of bird they want, in which case we know a little of what we are dealing with and then follow the normal procedure that we have evolved. Sadly we also get calls from people who just 'want a bird' not knowing what sort they want or why they really want it. The only criteria that seems to interest them are the different prices involved—preferably

wanting the cheapest bird available. This is not the right attitude to have to any living creature, yet in these cases when we ask why they want a bird, some callers get angry and upset. This is a great shame as it is not our intention to appear superior or unpleasant, we are only interested firstly in the welfare of the birds and, secondly, the welfare of falconry. We are also concerned that the person wanting the bird will eventually get the right one for him and the area in which he lives, thus giving the new bird and owner the chance of a long and happy relationship.

Have You Time?

The first question that anyone should ask themselves is whether they have the time to look after and fly a bird properly. During the initial training period you will need at least an hour of daylight per day. This is normally easy as young birds should be ready for training in summer when daylight hours are long. Once you have started hunting the time needed varies from one hour to five or six depending on how successful you are and the availability of quarry.

Never forget that although you may have planned just a quick hour's outing before getting to work or whatever, your bird may decide that this is the day it is going to be difficult and not return for several hours and perhaps not until the next day. This will leave you with a huge problem. Do you leave the bird and go to work hoping it will still be there on your return? This is unlikely, even if you are able to see anything in the pitch dark. Do you persevere with the bird and not get to work? How long will you keep your job, if this happens on a regular basis?

Still on the subject of time, how will your family feel if you are out hawking every weekend during the winter months? There is a high rate of divorce among falconers and if you care for your family, is it fair to spend all your time with a bird, albeit of the feathered kind?

You may have no family, no problems with lack of time because of your job, but what happens if you want to go on holiday? Do you take your bird with you, will the hotel appreciate crap all over the bedroom walls? In my experience they are, quite rightly, not over keen. Have you got a friend who is experienced in looking after birds and will have the bird for you and keep it safe? Is there someone experienced with whom you can leave your bird, and who will stay in your house while you are away, and if he has his own birds will he bring them with him? Are those birds healthy or might they bring a disease to your birds?

I had a telephone call from a lady in the Midlands one summer. She had been left with a Ferruginous Buzzard to look after, by her neighbour. The bird had got tangled in its chain and she was too

Connie at a frozen pond

frightened to handle it, but in the meantime it was injuring itself. I don't know why it was on a chain, but when she got somewhat unpleasant I did ask her why she had taken on the responsibility of a creature that she had no experience with and of which she was frightened. She expected me to leave here and drive up and help the bird. Eventually we managed to find a falconer close by to go and help it, but the problem should never have arisen. No falconer in his right mind should even consider asking someone who is not experienced in handling birds to care for his birds while he is away. The person solely responsible for that problem was the owner of the bird. Ask any bird-keeper when his birds usually decide to get ill, escape, get eaten by a fox or whatever; most of them will tell you that it is while they are away.

The time problems are endless and time itself must be given to thinking about how to deal with them. Don't think that I am trying to put people off falconry or generally keeping birds; I just want everyone to think ahead and look at possible problems before they arise. Think them out before committing yourself and your family, if you have one, to the time aspects of keeping a living bird.

Land; Have You Permission?

The next question to ask yourself, is can you get permission on local land to fly a bird at quarry. Unless you can do this there is little point in getting a bird to fly in the first place. Almost no landowner will give you permission to fly at pheasants for nothing, particularly if they are putting pheasants down for shooting. The only sensible way to have pheasant hunting is to do what the shooting people do and buy your own hunting rights. This is very costly and far beyond the pocket of most of us, although there is nothing to stop anyone getting together a syndicate of falconers and making the cost more reasonable. Much the same goes for partridges and grouse.

Rabbits however are a different matter and most farmers are pleased to have them caught. Still, whatever it is you are hunting remember that unless you are very lucky, the land is not yours. Most farmers think of their land as their garden and like to have it treated with respect. Think how you would feel if you gave someone permission to walk through your garden and they went straight over your flowerbed, left the gate open or broke the fences.

We nearly always phone or try to phone the people who are kind enough to let us fly on their land and tell them we are coming. Once the bird is going well enough for others to see something, we ask the landowner if he would like to come out and see the bird work. A Christmas bottle of whisky or gin does not come amiss as a thankyou for permission to use land. If the land is used badly and the owner feels misused, it will be to the detriment of all of us in the long run.

Can You Afford It?

Question three will have to be whether you can afford it. To keep a bird properly and safely you will need all the necessary equipment (see chapter 3). Going by 1992 prices a bird will cost you anything from £200 to £2000. A falconry course will also have to be paid for and the cheapest will almost certainly not be the best. The bird will need the services of a vet at sometime in its life.

Before starting in falconry, price it out. Remember building materials and labour, be it your own or someone else's. All of these are expensive, so price it just the way you price a car or a holiday or a new garage, then add another 10 per cent more for the buggeration factor.

What Type of Bird?

The type of bird you will end up with, if you decide to go this far is dictated not by what you want, but by what is most suitable for

the area you live in and intend flying the bird over. I would suggest
through experience that it is not a good idea to have hunting grounds
a very long way from where you live. This not only cuts down the
time out flying with the bird, which in turn cuts down on the bird's
fitness, but makes life very difficult if your bird gets lost and you
have to go miles to get to where it was last seen.

I sometimes wish that more notice was taken of what different
raptors do in the wild. If you look for example at Ferruginous
Buzzards you will find that they live in the open prairies, soaring a
great deal in strong winds and nesting either on very small juniper
trees, on the ground or on low rocky outcrops. Where they come
from there are no trees with branches like the usual trees over here,
they have all been stunted and the birds sit right on the tops. Yet I
have had people tell me that their bird is useless because it won't go
into trees and sits on the ground. That's what they are supposed to
do; they have spent thousands of years evolving to do just that as
they have had few other options.

A little research into the habits of any species of raptor in the
wild, will lead to a far greater understanding of the bird in captivity.
I am delighted to say that it does work the other way as well and
few ornithologists will ever have the intimate understanding that a
good falconer gets with a species worked with over a long period.

So look at the ground you hope to fly your bird over, look at
the quarry you hope to hunt and then find out what species will
fit into those categories. It is a good idea to also look at yourself
a little. If you are short on time or patience then it is best to forget
the true hawk families as they require a great deal of both. It is
always a good idea to match the temperament of the bird with the
temperament of the human.

Do You Want To Hunt?

I suppose another question should be, do you want to hunt with a
bird? There are now people who do not want to do this, but just
want to either fly a bird to the lure or have it as a pet. As a falconer I
really don't approve of this. Birds of prey hunt naturally, and if you
fly one this is the whole point—to see what the bird does naturally.
However I can understand what some people want to do, though if
this is the case they too should lay down some rules for themselves.

Firstly, if you are actively keeping a bird not to hunt and just
as a pet then you cannot call yourself a falconer. Remember that
although it is a pet to you, your bird may well not be a pet to others, and so you should only fly a bird where it will not upset other
members of the public. Nor is a good idea to take any bird of prey
through crowded places such as the local high street, not because it

is dangerous but because people tend not to expect birds of prey at close quarters in towns and can get upset or frightened. Such conduct can be irresponsible, and is not good for birds of prey in general.

There may be a time when your bird catches something. You must, then, be prepared to go in quickly and help it kill whatever it has caught, even if you don't hunt because you don't like killing. That is your responsibility and, if you don't take that responsibility, you should not have the bird.

The number of birds that will take to pet-keeping are very few. I would say that only Kestrels and Common Buzzards are suitable (remembering that I generally do not approve anyway). These two species are pretty lazy, and given a good supply of food will not normally bother to hunt if no effort is made on the part of the owner. I do not think owls make good pets once they are adult.

Whatever bird you want and whatever the reason you want it, the subject should be researched properly first. The same should be done if you wish to take up captive breeding. Most of the information required is to be found if you look for it. Then when you have researched and know roughly what is involved ask yourself 'Is it for me'?

Egyptian Vulture

10 CONSERVATION

While I was thinking about this chapter, I was going through all
the ways I could defend falconry and put it in a fairer light than it
has had recently. But I actually believe there is nothing to defend.
It is, in Britain, a perfectly legal sport and most of us are doing it
perfectly legally. The same can be said of the United States and most
other countries where falconry is legal. So, to all those people who
try to force falconry into a defensive position, I rather feel like saying
balls to the lot of them, but I suppose I had better not. Falconry has
had the most enormous amount of bad publicity and so, given the
chance to get something in print, I should not lose the opportunity
to put the record a little straighter.

There is no species of raptor in the world that has been, or is, to
date, being threatened by falconry. If we look back into history, we
find that many more birds were taken from the wild in this country
for falconry during the Middle Ages than have ever been taken this
century, yet no species suffered a decline. Indeed, far more destructive
things have happened to birds of prey over the centuries in terms of
persecution and it would be fair to say that breeding populations were
not affected until after World War II, when the arrival of synthetic
chemical pesticides and the start of wholesale destruction of tropical
forests and other natural habitats, began to cause serious environ-
mental problems. Yet when I ask visitors to The NBoP Centre if they
know why the Peregrine, for example, became rare in Britain, almost
all of them blame falconers or egg collectors. This is mainly because
of the massive and inaccurate propaganda put out by the press and
bird societies. In truth, the Peregrine was brought to a low ebb by
the pesticide DDT. It is not only no longer rare in Britain but has,
since the voluntary ceasing of the use of DDT in this country, made
one of the most successful recoveries of any animal put in peril.

There has always been the most amazing rubbish spoken about the Peregrine, particularly in the press. I have suffered myself, from lack of research for the truth, in a *Sunday Times* article. It seems that newspapers like to find a story that lends itself to drama and use it regardless of the effect. I suppose the thing that upsets me the most is the fact that I can see no good as regards the conserving of Peregrines, or any other bird of prey, coming out of this sort of journalism. It does nothing for conservation.

Birds of prey are not exactly cheap, but they have never fetched the sort of monies that have been suggested by the spate of publicity world-wide. Nor, when you add up the total costs of captive breeding are birds so overpriced in real terms.

Occasionally a Saker will fetch a lot of money from an Arab buyer in the Pakistan markets, when it is a large, particularly beautiful passage bird of very pale colour, and even more so if more than one person wants the bird. Then it becomes a matter of prestige to be its owner. But the prices quoted by bird societies and newspapers are mostly founded on excellent imaginations and little else.

It is interesting to note that over 90 per cent of the world's breeding schemes for birds of prey have been started by people with an interest in falconry. These are often run by falconers. The offspring from many of these breeding projects are willingly and lovingly released, and it gives many falconers great joy to see such success, contrary to those people who are convinced that falconers are only interested in seeing birds in captivity.

Being open to the public, one has a much greater chance to see how the public react to falconry and the keeping of birds generally. There can be no doubt that the general public are much more aware about wildlife now than previously. Anyone keeping wildlife in captivity has to be very careful to do so well, and with just reason.

We fall between two stools here because basically we are a specialist zoo, containing nothing but birds of prey, but we also are falconers ourselves and employ falconry methods to train our birds and fly them during demonstrations for the visitors. I think sometimes the visitors get confused, and many say how they don't like zoos but enjoy coming to visit us here. Yet, we are a zoo. Not all our birds are flown by any means. The majority of them are in pens for breeding, albeit in pens that are improving all the time, and our success rate is high. People love to see the birds fly, but are worried about seeing them tethered. On the other hand, the tethered birds are sometimes very close to the public with no wire between them and the watching visitor which is wonderful for photography, and the visitors love being able to see them at such close quarters.

By being open to the public we share our collection with them and because we are always available to talk to the visitors particu-

larly during and after flying demonstrations, we have a wonderful opportunity to put over what we feel about conservation. We get very good feedback about how people feel concerning the job we are trying to do. This tends to keep one on one's toes, which is excellent for anyone working in the conservation field. It is important to have to explain what you are trying to do because it not only gets the message across, but makes you think about the pros and cons of what you are doing, and if you are doing it right, on a very regular basis.

It is the responsibility of all falconers to understand the need to explain to interested bystanders what is being done and why. Not to justify, nor to tell how, merely to explain. Some falconers think, mistakenly, that it is better to make falconry appear very difficult and perhaps mystical, thinking this will put off people who might be interested in taking up the sport. In fact, very often this has the reverse effect. We found the best way to put people off starting was to teach them how to do it—show them all that is entailed, preferably in the winter when it is cold and miserable and the bird still has to be flown and cared for, even when one's hand is almost frozen in the glove and a bird landing hard is positively painful. Then only those who are genuinely interested will continue and those who thought they might like to start, have learnt a great deal, hopefully had an enjoyable time and decided against starting. I always take my hat off to these people who have obviously learnt the real message on a falconry course, which is only take it up if you are in a position to do so properly.

As said before, falconry has not and is unlikely ever to have any detrimental effect on wild species of raptor, but it has had many beneficial side effects. As well as the enormous advances in the knowledge of raptor diseases, there are now many more vets interested in birds of prey. Both these facts are, in great part, due to the numbers of captive and injured wild birds brought to them by falconers. A very high percentage of those people who take in, treat and care for injured wild birds from the public are falconers. Insight into the behaviour and habits of birds of prey has come from falconers, who have the chance to get to know a potentially wild bird in a way that no scientist can.

Falconry gives a great deal of pleasure to an increasing number of people, and at a point in our history when mankind is going through some pretty uneasy and worrying times. Unemployment, poor education and often lack of ambition means that many people go through life with little to interest them, becoming television addicts at best, and gaining addiction to much more dangerous products at worst. I believe that if wild populations are unaffected and captive

Heidi and I having a bath!

Help with conservation is needed from everyone. The Princess Royal opened our Eagle Barn in June, 1987. Now foster parent to two pairs of Barn Owls, she is seen here explaining the complexities of audio-directional technology—'It's over there!'

populations are happy, flown and well cared for, falconry is a good thing if controlled. Those who would like to see it banned usually have little experience or understanding of the relationships that can be formed between man and animals. In fact it always seems a shame to me that the various anti brigades could not put their undeniable energy into realistic conservation projects and efforts, rather than trying to stop something that has been a part of mankind for centuries—involvement with wildlife.

To be a conservationist in the sense that I hope I try to be means that one must be an optimist. When looking at the countless problems that affect the conserving of our world as it is today, it would be very easy to give up, to say that what 'I' do is of such insignificance that it cannot possibly have any long-term effect or results would probably be very close to the truth. But it is not the attitude any of us can afford to have. The more of us there are who try and do a little bit, however small and however insignificant, the more it adds up.

I wish there wasn't a division between those who call themselves falconers and those who call themselves conservationists. However, it is there at the moment and although it upsets me, I will have to talk in terms of this division as I can find no other words that I can use. I would term myself as being both, a falconer and a conservationist, flying birds for hunting (although not often right now I will admit), and running a Centre that is open to the public, endeavouring to manage captive breeding, release and educational schemes. There are many conservationists who would disagree with me. They would say that falconers put pressure on wild populations of birds of prey, and are generally anti-conservation, only wanting birds of prey in captivity.

Very often falconers are their own worst enemies, not always having the political awareness to cope in the right way at the right time with some of the accusations thrown at them. There are among falconers a group which flout the law, and take birds and eggs illegally regardless of the long-term damage done to the reputation of other more genuine falconers and the sport itself. These people very obviously don't have either their fellow falconers' or the sport's welfare at heart. Conservationists love this unpleasant faction in falconry as it hands them ammunition on a plate. There are, and always will be, conservationists who would like to see the sport of falconry banned and the keeping of birds of prey made illegal. They grab at bad publicity on falconers or the sport and use it for all they are worth.

Some falconers deny that the bad element are actually true falconers, but this is a poor argument and in many cases not true. To wash one's hands of the less desirable in one's own field of work, interests or hobbies is the escapist's way out and no argument in defence of that sport or hobby. In every facet of life there are good and bad elements. There are bad policemen, teachers, doctors, scientists, dentists, conservationists and so on. Falconers don't believe that the poor among these groups are not real teachers, scientists etc; they fully realise that for every bad one there are probably hundreds of good ones. Perhaps those who constantly tar all falconers with the same brush should be more open-minded.

Because of my personal interest in conservation, I go to conferences on birds of prey all over the world. I was really excited when going to my first one, thinking of meeting all these people who were as interested in raptors as I and talking to them. But I was wrong. Many were not in the slightest bit interested in sharing information, particularly with someone from a non-scientific background who had no official letters after her name. How could anyone know anything at all about birds of prey if she did not have at least one scientific degree and preferably more?

I was, at the end of it, very disillusioned and upset. But I was glad in the long run that it happened. It took about six months before I had thought the whole thing through and got over it. But I learned a great deal. I learned that you have to be politically aware to work in the conservation field. That many scientists don't particularly like to talk to non-scientists, but that they also have to work hard to get the funding they need to earn a living and carry out the research that interests them. And that some of them are wonderful people who have over the intervening years become my good friends.

But most important I learned that until falconers, scientists, bird societies and all others with an interest in birds of prey all over the world learn to agree to disagree over some points, all of them relatively unimportant, realise that the long-term aims of each group are roughly the same, and learn to work together, conservation will be very much the poorer. The real enemies of birds of prey are economics, politics and culture. All those aspects of the world need to be tackled with unity and the 'in fighting' among conservationists must stop before it is too late and we have nothing left to conserve.

Conservation should be part of everyone's daily life, and starts in everyone's home, although most people prefer to ignore that fact. We cannot even blame our poor record in conservation worldwide on ignorance, but on apathy. We in the First World can no longer say that we do not see the dangers in polluting the world, in denuding it of life-giving, oxygen-giving plants or destroying our very atmosphere with such mundane things as aerosol sprays. We have been told, the warnings are there, and yet we choose to ignore them. How many of us have given up using the dangerous aerosol sprays rather than use the good ones around the house, or refuse to use up the world's hardwoods in our homes as front doors, windows, kitchen furniture—even throwing away old but perfectly serviceable furniture to do so. Do we look to see where our products come from so that, for example, we could put economic pressure on the Japanese to stop them fishing out all our oceans before it is too late? How many of us are looking into using lead-free petrol in our cars? The lists are endless and all relevant to most of us in our everyday lives. Perhaps you would prefer just to wait until all these things are either banned, or the natural products just run out. This is of course the easy way, the apathetic and, shamefully, the normal way.

If you say that you like birds of prey, for example, or want to be a falconer or a bird watcher or a conservationist, there are thousands of things that every such human in the world can do in small ways to help conserve not only birds of prey, but the whole ecosystem.

Without this delicate and beautiful ecosystem mankind will finally pass into the extinction he has so justly earned, sadly and unforgivably taking with him all other living things that did not earn and do not deserve that end.

11 THE FUTURE

As I said at the start of this book, falconry has changed and it is time for falconers to change with it. Many have already, some still have to catch up with the 1990s. Change does not necessarily mean for the worse; many changes in falconry have been very much for the better. Who would go back to flying birds without telemetry once they have learned to use it well; or want to lose the veterinary knowledge we have gained? Where would falconry be without captive breeding?

The people in falconry have changed too. It is a much broader spectrum that partake these days, but that is no bad thing. New people and fresh views are good for the sport, as long as the birds are well looked after and flown very regularly.

I can almost hear some people crying out how commercialism is ruining falconry. For heaven's sake grow up, you people—what could we have done without it? Where would the incentive have been to get as far as we have in the field of captive breeding? No one in their right mind would be spending the amount of time and money that is now being spent on producing birds for no return. Anyone who does not believe that is, I guarantee, someone who either breeds nothing and consequently knows nothing of the costs or else is rich and can afford not to count them. If the costs were really added up, taking into consideration the amount of time and money invested, then captive breeding is only just beginning to pay for itself.

I would like to think that falconry does have a future in this country. There are countries where falconry has been banned. There are countries where falconry is illegal. Its future in Britain has been shaky at times, but falconry is stabilising now with the 1984 legislation and with captive breeding. The future of falconry here now lies in the behaviour of those people partaking in the sport, the success of captive breeding, the availability of land and quarry, and, probably the most risky aspect of all, the continuance of legal field sports.

It is up to all of us in falconry now and those who come into it in the future, to make sure that we behave, not only within the laws, but within certain moral codes—not some of the very out-dated codes in the existing clubs, but a code that ensures the safety of falconry for future generations. There must be respect and enjoyment of the quarry and due regard to land and landowners. Thoughtful caring falconers must look after their birds well and hunt them regularly, keeping them happy and a credit to the sport. That includes old birds who have served well and deserve in their retirement also to be served

Conservation is expensive. If sponsorship can help, it should not be frowned upon. Peter Dominic sponsored me for five years

I would like to think that falconry does have a future

well. I would like to see the end of people overburdened with birds that they cannot possibly fly regularly and are not trying to breed with.

Breeders of captive birds should make sure that they behave responsibly, breeding good birds, and trying to ensure good, knowledgeable homes. Wherever possible they should not use or sell siblings as breeding pairs, thus causing possible problems in the future.

Those teaching falconry should advise people when they are and when they are not suitable to carry on further in the sport. Those in front of the public should not over-encourage people to start falconry, nor exaggerate the powers and dangers of raptors in general.

Falconry has enough potential enemies; there are many that would like still to see it banned. So most important, apart from the welfare of the birds, falconers should, like the conservationists, forget their arguments or differences and pull together to make sure that their sport does indeed have a future.

BIBLIOGRAPHY
AND USEFUL ADDRESSES

Anderson Brown, Dr A. F. *The Incubation Book* (Saiga Publishing).

Beebe and Webster. *North American Falconry and Hawking.*

Burton, John A. *Owls of the World* (Peter Lowe).

Cade, T. J. *The Falcons of the World* (Collins).

Coles, B. H. *Avian Medicine and Surgery* (Blackwell).

Cooper, J. E. and Eley, J. T. *First Aid and Care of Wild Birds* (David & Charles).

Cooper, J. E. and Greenwood, A. G. *Recent Advances in the Study of Raptor Diseases* (Chiron Publishing).

Cooper, J. E. *Veterinary Aspects of Captive Birds of Prey* (Standfast Press).

Ford, Emma. *Birds of Prey* (Batsford).

Glasier, P. *Falconry and Hawking* (Batsford).

Llewellyn, P., and Brain, P. *Assessing Condition Prior to Raptor Release in Breeding and Management in Birds of Prey*, Proceedings of the Conference held at Bristol University, January 1987 (Bristol University).

Parry-Jones, J. *Birds of Prey* (The National Birds of Prey Centre).

The Peregrine Fund *Falcon Propogation* (The Peregrine Fund, USA).

All the above books have been used for reference, and would be of great interest to anyone wishing to further their knowledge on the subject.

Licensing and Registration Authorities

Wildlife Licensing Department, Department of the Environment, Tollgate House, Houlton Street, Bristol BS2 9DJ. Tel: 0272 218649.

(Import/Export Health Certificate): Ministry of Agriculture, Fisheries and Food, Import/Export Section, Hook Rise South, Tolworth, Surbiton, Surrey KT6 7NF. Tel: 081 330 8222.

(As above, for Scotland): Department of Agriculture and Fisheries for Scotland, Pentlend House, 47 Robbs Loen, Edinburgh EH14 1SQ. Tel: 031 556 8400.

Telemetry

Martin Jones, The Lodge, Huntley, Glos GL19 3HG. Tel: 0452 830629.

Equipment Suppliers: Martin Jones (address as above)

Books

The National Birds of Prey Centre, Newent, Glos GL18 1JJ. Tel: 0531 820286.
Martin Jones (address as above)

Veterinary Surgeons Specialising in Birds of Prey

Neil Forbes MRCVS BVet Med, Lansdown Veterinary Group, The Clockhouse Veterinary Hospital, Wallbridge Road, Stroud, Glos GL5 3JD. Tel: 0453 672555.
A. Greenwood, Moorhouse Farm, Moorhouse Lane, Oxenhope, Keighley, West Yorkshire BD22 9RX. Tel: 0535 42982.
C. Watson MA Vet MB MRCVS, Wood Veterinary Group, 124 Stroud Road, Glos. Tel: 0452 20056.
N. Harcourt Brown BVSc, 30 Crab Lane, Bilton, Harrowgate, N. Yorks. Tel: 0423 508945.
M. Williams BVSc MRCVS, 11 New Street, Upton on Severn, Worcs. Tel: 0684 592606.
S. Spencer BVSc MRCVS, Maison Dieu Veterinary Centre, Maison Dieu Road, Dover, Kent CT16 1RE. Tel: 0304 201617.

Falconry Courses

British School of Falconry, Stelling Minnis, Canterbury, Kent CT4 6AQ. Tel: 0227 87575.
Hawksport, Rose Cottage, Bury Bar Lane, Newent, Glos GL18 1PT. Tel: 0531 821573.
Scottish Academy of Falconry, Bonchester Bridge, Hawick, Roxburghshire TD9 9TB. Tel: 045086 666.

General

The British Field Sports Society, 59 Kennington Road, London SE1 7PZ. Tel: 071 928 4742.

The Hawk and Owl Trust, Blickling Hall, Aylsham, Norwich, Norfolk NR11 6NF.
The Hawk Conservancy, Weyhill, Nr Andover, Hants SP11 8DY. Tel: 026477 2252.
The Hawk Board, Secretary Sue Dewar, 6 Glendevon Road, Woodley, Reading, Berkshire RG5 4PH. Tel: 0734 696501.

Falconry Clubs

British Falconers Club (branches all over Britain): Home Farm, Tamworth, Staffordshire B78 3DW.
Welsh Hawking Club: Aendy Farmhouse, Church Village, Pontypridd, Glamorgan, Wales.

Falconry Demonstrations, Lectures, Talks, Courses

The National Birds of Prey Centre, Newent, Gloucestershire GL18 1JJ. Tel: 0531 820286; Fax: 0531 821389.

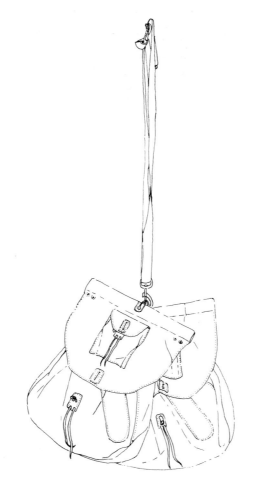

ACKNOWLEDGEMENTS

I would like to thank all those who have helped me with photographs—Eric and David Hosking, Peter Knight and Marion McCourt without whose help I would have had very few, as I am one of the world's worst photographers; Neil and Cheryl Davis who did all the illustrations, and IBM for their word-processor which saved time and reams of paper. Also I would like to thank my husband Jo and our staff for doing all the things I should have been doing while writing this book.

Bramble

INDEX

Page numbers in *italic* indicate illustrations